HOME
WINE WAITER

HOME
WINE WAITER

Rosalind Cooper

HAMLYN

© Text Rosalind Cooper

Published 1985 by Hamlyn Publishing,
a division of The Hamlyn Publishing Group Limited,
Bridge House, London Road, Twickenham, Middlesex, England

Designed and produced by Nicholas Enterprises Limited,
70 Old Compton Street, London W1

© Copyright Nicholas Enterprises Limited 1985

ISBN 0600 32509 1

Printed in Italy by Arti Grafiche Vincenzo Bona - Torino

CONTENTS

INTRODUCTION

More people are drinking wine worldwide than ever before, and more and more people are becoming knowledgeable about it. While this trend is admirable, there are still a great number of people who enjoy drinking wine but are put off by the mystique surrounding the subject—especially when it comes to discussing 'fine' wines and the relative merits of certain vintages!

This informative book is for the everyday drinker, not the connoisseur. It assumes that the reader generally buys wine in a supermarket or wine store where he or she hopes to get good value for money. Usually, the wines come from a variety of countries, not just France, Germany and Italy, traditionally considered the best wine producers. This is why this book discusses styles of wine—white wines, red wines,

sparkling wines and fortified wines— rather than geographical regions, in order to help you make choices in a more practical way. It tells you how to read a wine label so that you know precisely what you are buying; and you will learn about serving wine and which food best complements different types. For readers who wish to increase their knowledge of wine, the dictionary section of WINES AND VINES includes basic information about the world's best-known wines and wine-producing regions and a reference section at the end of the book lists the classifications of French Bordeaux and Burgundy wines.

We hope that this book will encourage you to experiment with wine and wine tasting and above all to enjoy choosing and drinking wine.

WHAT IS WINE?

Trefethen vineyards, Napa Valley, California

GEWÜRZT

9

B A S I C S   O F   W I N E

We are living in a golden age for wine-lovers. There is a greater choice of wines available than ever before and the quality standards, thanks to modern technology combined with long experience, are now reliably high.

It is important to remember that wine is an entirely natural product. Anything added to wine is usually natural too, such as a little sulphur as a preservative. As we try to live healthier lives and we become more aware of what we eat and drink, wine can play a real role in our lifestyle.

Wine almost makes itself. The very first wine may have been made by accident when some shepherd took grapes with him to the fields and left them in a leather bag until they began to ferment. After a very short time this fermentation would produce a simple kind of alcoholic liquid – the most basic type of wine.

The usual definition of wine is that it is the 'fermented juice of freshly gathered grapes'. What could be simpler than that? The crushed grapes have yeast on their skins and this acts on the sugar in the juice to bring about a change which produces alcohol. And at the same time a great deal of the flavour of the grape is preserved, along with subtler characteristics which experts claim give wines their value in terms of flavour and price.

So why are some wines red and others white or pink? It is easy to understand the distinction: red wines are made using the skins of the grapes and white are made from juice only.

R E D   W I N E

To make red wine, the juice is pressed from black grapes and left in contact with the dark skins during the fermentation process. This gives the wine its colour and adds a certain 'texture' to a red wine, making it a little heavier in style than a typical white wine. The heavy quality is due to a substance called *tannin* which comes from the skins and also from the wood of the barrels often used in ageing wine. If a red wine is not aged in wood, it will have a much fruitier and lighter taste, similar to a white wine. A good example of this style of red wine is **Beaujolais** from France.

W H I T E   W I N E S

These are the popular favourites of our age and the preferred style is often quite dry. White wines have a pleasant fruity quality. They

taste of the grape they are made from, and are rarely aged in wood. They still ferment naturally because the yeasts are passed from the skins to the juice during the pressing of the grapes. In general, white wines are slightly lower in alcohol than red wines and lack the harsher elements which are intriguing to wine buffs, but can be alarming to the novice. Remember that the juice of almost all grapes is colourless and a white wine may easily be made from red (black) grapes. The fermentation process is generally controlled today, often by means of refrigeration. A sweeter wine is made from ripe grapes and the fermentation is stopped before all the sugar in the grapes has turned into alcohol. A sweet wine may have some added sugar. A medium-dry wine is one which has some sweetness but is not a dessert wine.

ROSÉ WINES

These pretty pink wines can be very pleasant with picnics and on warm days. They may be sweet, medium or dry in style depending on how they were fermented. The colour comes from leaving the skins of red grapes in contact with the juice for a short time. Occasionally a rosé wine is made by mixing (blending) a red and white wine, but this is never the case with a quality wine. Many rosé wines are sold in attractive and unusual containers which contribute to their image as 'fun' wines.

SPARKLING WINES

A sparking wine may be made in any wine region of the world simply by 'catching' the gas released when wine ferments. During the process carbon dioxide gas is given off. If it cannot escape, it remains in the wine as those delicious bubbles we associate with **Champagne** and other fine sparkling wines. The name Champagne may only be used in Europe to mean the very special wines made in a small region of that name in northern France. Keeping those bubbles is a lengthy and expensive business and the method used is called *méthode champenoise*. This method is also used in other wine areas such as California and Spain to make some very good quality sparklers. Cheaper versions are made either by bubbling up the wine in special tanks or by adding carbon dioxide.

　　Use price as your guide when choosing a sparkling wine. If it isn't champagne then check for the words *méthode champenoise*. Beware the cheapest version as this could be all fizz and no flavour. The finer sparkling wines release their bubbles just a little at a time. If you prefer a sweeter style, look for the name *Rich* on the label; a medium-dry European sparkler will be described as *Demi-sec* or even *Sec* (which is confusing as *sec* actually means 'dry' in French); and the drier style is known as *Brut* or *Dry*. A sparkling wine may be white or red, and rosé champagne is highly prized.

Cheaper rosé sparkling wines are often very sweet, such as **Cold Duck** which is so popular in Canada.

F O R T I F I E D   W I N E S

The major names here are **vermouth**, **sherry** and **port**, but **madeira** and **marsala** wines are also quite important. They are known as 'fortified' because grape brandy is added. Sometimes, as is the case with port, this is done before fermentation is complete, so the wine remains sweet. A typical fortified wine is about half as strong as standard spirits such as whisky and gin.

Adding brandy improves a dull or rough wine. Then it is aged in wood casks or in glass containers to make it smoother. **Vintage port** is prized by connoisseurs but there are many cheaper ports including the **ruby** and **tawny** styles which are excellent value for the money. Most port is red but there is also a white port. As with champagne, the real thing comes from one special area of Europe – in this case northern Portugal – but good port is also made in California and South Africa.

Sherry originates from the town of Jerez in Spain, but is also made in Cyprus, Australia, South Africa and California. The main styles are pale and dry (called *fino* in Spanish); medium-dry (called *amontillado);* or dark and sweet (called *oloroso).* The very popular cream sherries are rich olorosos, which may be either pale or dark in colour.

Vermouth is essential for the cocktail cabinet. It is simply a wine flavoured with a variety of herbs with grape brandy added. **Madeira** comes from the island of that name and is made using a heating process which 'bakes' the wine before it is fortified, giving it a pungent flavour. **Marsala** is usually very sweet and is much used in cooking, as is madeira.

H O W   S T R O N G   I S   W I N E ?

Many wines these days list their alcohol content on their label. A typical table wine will have an alcoholic strength of about 10-14 degrees, a fortified wine about 15-20 degrees. (Note: these measures are according to the European Gay-Lussac or GL scale; in the US the equivalent would be 20 to 40 proof.)

A bottle of wine usually holds either 70 or 75 centilitres. (three-quarters of a litre) and will serve approximately six glasses. Each glass is around 100 calories assuming the wine is a normal-strength table wine, or more for a fortified wine. So a glass of wine is equivalent in strength to a single measure of spirits in a bar (4 cl.) or one can of beer (27.5 cl. on average).

S E R V I N G   W I N E

A great deal of nonsense is written and said about serving wine. Some people claim that you need all kinds of fancy decanters and elegant glassware in order to appreciate wine and that the serving temperature needs to be as closely calculated as a medical chart. Of course this is exaggeration.

What has happened is that some pleasant traditions connected with serving wine in restaurants and at dinner parties have been adopted as the norm for everyday use at home. You need only visit France or Italy to see that this is not necessary. In those celebrated wine-growing countries they serve wine as part of a meal without fuss or ceremony.

Make sure you have a supply of fair-sized wine glasses on hand. These should be made of clear glass and preferably have a stem. Keep your wines in a fairly cool place which is undisturbed as wines do not like vibration or sudden changes of temperature. The storage place also ought to be dimly lit.

Select the wine you plan to serve at lunch or dinner in advance, using the guidelines in the following sections of this book to help your choice.

White or sparkling wine Chill in the refrigerator for at least two hours before the meal then, if possible, transfer it to an ice bucket filled with a mixture of ice and water at the time of serving. Few wines can stand being really chilled. In the old days when wines were usually stored in cool cellars the temperature was ideal. Today we can duplicate those conditions using the ice bucket technique and get the best from white wines and from sparkling wines.

Use a well-made corkscrew to open your bottle. Never use one that pumps air into the wine as this can be dangerous. A white wine is opened just as you serve it. Sparkling wine is opened by removing the foil and the wire, then wrapping the bottle in a clean cloth and turning the bottle gently while holding the cork until it releases with a gentle 'pop' – not an explosive bang. To add a little glamour to the occasion, serve these wines in glasses which have been frosted by placing them in the freezer for a short time before the moment of service.

Rosé wines These should be treated in a similar fashion but served cool rather than cold. Bring them out of the refrigerator before serving and transfer to an ice bucket. There are also red wines which benefit from being served cool – these include **Beaujolais** from France and **Lambrusco** from Italy.

Red wines As a general rule, a red wine needs to be served at cool room temperature. The average centrally-heated room is too hot, so serve at about 18°C (65°F) wherever possible.

One point to remember about all wines, and especially reds, is that they are still 'living' in the bottle, changing and reacting to the air until the moment they are consumed. That's why a freezer is a shock for a white wine and a heated room can be too hot for a good

Using the 'waiter's friend' corkscrew

red wine. You may have read about 'letting a wine breathe' by decanting or simply opening it ahead of time. Oddly enough, this is very useful for ordinary red wines which may have a harsh taste. A young inexpensive red wine will taste smoother if it is served at the right temperature and opened at least an hour beforehand. But be cautious with any wine of more than 10 years old – open too early and all that delicate flavour could be lost. With the exception of some heavy Rhônes wines like **Châteauneuf du Pape** and some rich Italian or California reds like **Barbera** the maximum time of airing should be two hours.

Decanting wine By all means use a decanter or carafe if you prefer. To decant, simply pour the wine from the bottle steadily into the decanter. Use a plastic funnel if you doubt the steadiness of your hand, or hold the decanter over the sink to avoid drips. Watch the last inch of wine at the bottom of the bottle as there could be some sediment (the deposit found at the bottom of some bottles of red wine, particularly those which are well-aged or full-bodied). Keep the bottle well-lit (this was once done by the light of a candle by British butlers) and leave those dregs in the bottle.

Fortified wines Vintage port always has a sediment and it seems a shame to waste any of this port – use a coffee filter to extract the last few drops of nectar! Serve all ports at room temperature except for white port, which may be served with ice. Similarly, most sherries are traditionally served at room temperature, but today they are often offered over ice and taste just as good this way. Fino is always chilled before serving. Other fortified wines are normally offered at room temperature but there are no hard and fast rules – use your judgement based on the weather and the tastes of your guests. Fortified wines have so much flavour that they can stand a touch of ice without any dilution of taste.

But it is not a good idea to ice table wines because they taste watery and unpleasant after a few moments. Mix an inexpensive white wine with soda or orange juice to make a cooling long drink.

WHY SOME WINES ARE FINE

There is usually a very good reason for the price differential between the various wines on the market. Price is related to the complexity of the wine, and its availability. The most basic style of wine, often called *table* or *'jug'* wine, is made using the benefits of modern technology. This type of wine is mass-produced to taste reliably agreeable and consistent.

Next are the 'local' wines which have a certain regional character and charm but are not in any way elegant. Many of the Italian wines are of this type, including **Valpolicella**, **Chianti** and **Soave**. The **Vin de Pays** wines of France and the red and white **Rioja** of Spain are also this type. Once you have decided which of these wines suits you they are excellent for everyday.

One step up from these regional wines are those from particular châteaux or villages, although not the really famous ones, which are of interest to the wine buff. This type of mid-priced wine can be tricky to select. You should use the WINES AND VINES section to aid you here.

Finally, there are all the so-called 'fine' wines, including such legendary names as **Schloss Johannisberg**, **Château Latour**, **Romanée-Conti** and **Krug** (champagne). Some of the rarest of these wines, like **Château Pétrus** from the Bordeaux region of France, are so expensive that they attract investors rather than drinkers – the wine is too valuable to drink. But others can be within your reach if you choose a less renowned vintage or find a shipper who is less well known. As with all luxury products, these wines are a triumph of marketing and may not be worth the money you pay. However, they have great snob appeal.

At the same time these wines are made with loving care to extremely high standards and then kept until almost mature in cask or bottle at the cellar or château where they are made. In the case of **champagne**, each bottle must be carefully turned daily by hand for several weeks before the sediment from a secondary fermenting process can be removed and the champagne becomes the crystal clear wine we know. All this labour costs a great deal, as does the storage, when local governments tax wine producers on each bottle or cask stored. Just imagine the cellars of **Moët & Chandon**, for instance, where an average of 25 million bottles of champagne are resting at any one time.

Generally you do get what you pay for in wine as with any other purchase. Give yourself time to develop your taste and preferences, and don't be afraid to ask your wine supplier for help. Use this book as a reference when you see an unfamiliar name or want to try something new.

Clarifying wine prior to bottling, Médoc, France

TALKING ABOUT WINE

Often the jargon of wine puts people off. Many budding wine enthusiasts have had their interest dampened by attending a wine tasting or picking up a specialist magazine where they find wines described in what seems like another language or even a secret code. Words like 'velvety nose' or 'aroma of violets and raspberries' sound odd and inappropriate to the uninitiated.

Even the idea of a wine tasting seems frightening. Will you have to spit out your samples, and, if so, where? Will your inexperience show when you discuss the wines? Wouldn't it be better to stick to a quiet drink at home?

And this principle applies to meals out as well. So many of us are intimidated by sommeliers brandishing a wine list embossed with leather, and lose our ability to choose a wine. Then we find he has selected something very expensive on our behalf. Or we visit an acquaintance and are offered a rather dull wine at dinner which he praises to the skies. We start to feel that our judgement is at fault, not the wine itself.

Another problem arises at the wine store. There we are confronted with all those bottles and no clue how to make a selection.

Fear not. Here is a brief introduction to the language of wine which will get you through any of these situations.

Bottle shapes: Straight-sided, high-shouldered bottles for Bordeaux wines (clear glass for sweet white wines); sloping shoulders for Burgundy and Loire wines; tall bottles for German wines, green for Mosel, brown for Rhine.

GETTING ACQUAINTED

As explained in the previous section, a wine will be either red, white, rosé or sparkling.

Red wine may also be called *rouge* (French), *rosso* (Italian), or *tinto* (Spanish or Portuguese). As many wine bottles are green (this helps to preserve the wine by protecting it from excessive sunlight) it is often hard to tell the exact colour of wine just by looking at it in the bottle.

White wine is also known as *blanc* (French), *bianco* (Italian), or *blanco* (Spanish). Some white wines are sold in clear glass to display their attractive colour, but they should be kept away from direct sunlight which will affect their flavour. Avoid any bottles in the store window for the same reason.

Rosé wine uses its French name in English-speaking countries but could also be labelled *rosato* (Italian), or *rosado* (Spanish). Of course, the international brands like **Mateus Rosé** always use English on their label with a view to the export markets.

SWEET AND DRY

After colour, the next vital consideration is whether a wine is sweet or dry. Some wines are traditionally always very dry (many red wines and certain white wines such as **Muscadet** or **Chablis** from France) or very rich and sweet (white **Sauternes** from France or *Auslese* wines from Germany). With these, the label is not always very helpful so refer to the WINES AND VINES section of this book to help you identify the differences.

But many wines are identified according to relative sweetness. Some stores even code their wines by a system of numbers indicating sweetness. Key words to watch for include:

Dry – may also be *sec* (French), *trocken* (German), *secco* (Italian or *seco* (Spanish).

Medium dry – could be *demi-sec* (French) or *amabile* (Italian).

Sweet – *doux* in French, *dolce* in Italian, *dulce* or *doce* in Spanish and Portuguese.

Quality wines are sealed with lead capsules while cheaper wines have capsules of thick plastic.

EXPRESSING JUDGEMENTS ON WINE: SOME USEFUL PHRASES

It pays to show confidence when talking about wine. Try to use some of the key phrases below. The first two are positive remarks which will flatter any host or hostess and sound just right to a wine waiter's ear.

This wine has an excellent finish – means that it has a quality of taste which lingers in the mouth even after drinking. See the next section for more details of 'finish' in connection with tasting wines.

This is a well-balanced wine – the ultimate compliment. Just like human beings, at certain stages of their lives wines are particularly attractive and agreeable! A well-balanced wine need not be expensive but it should have an interesting taste which has no rough edges and yet is not dull and insipid. Technically, the balance is between the fruit of the grapes and the extra flavour given by ageing the wine in wood or glass, but trust your own judgement on this one and don't let the 'experts' confuse you.

A wine of character – this is a very useful catch-all comment which is safe to use for any wine you like and which has a definite flavour.

A 'hot-country' wine – used to describe any wine which has a faint aroma of tar, or the smell of burnt raisins which comes from very ripe or even overripe grapes. Hot country wines are made in the South of France, California south of the Napa Valley, and in Australia and South America.

A classic wine – any of the 'fine' wines usually from a particular château or village. These are rarely cheap and cost upward of $10 or £7.

An interesting wine – means it is your host's choice, but not necessarily yours.

A full-bodied wine – most full-bodied wines are red and quite high in alcohol content. See the following section on TASTING for more help with this phrase. As a rule, a full-bodied wine has a flavour which stays with you after sipping and which stands up to foods which are quite pungent (e.g. French red **Burgundy, California Zinfandel**).

A delicate wine – the opposite of a full-bodied wine. This is normally applied to light white wine such as **Chablis** or **Riesling**. Sometimes a full-bodied wine is referred to as 'masculine' and a delicate wine as 'feminine' though these terms may not find favour with all lady wine tasters!

A lively wine – this can mean several things. Either the wine is actually sparkling, hence lively in the glass, or perhaps it has a slight 'prickle' on the tongue, as intended by the winemaker in **Chianti** from Italy, for example. Alternatively something might be starting to go wrong with the wine and this has caused the bubbles.

This wine needs time – means that the wine is still relatively young and could be kept for a while before drinking to improve its taste. Understanding when a wine is ready for drinking is difficult, but as a rule a red wine which is considered fine usually needs time.

The wine is corked – a vital phrase for quoting to the wine waiter or using in your wine store, but be very sure the wine really is undrinkable. A corked wine tastes of mouldy cork and is definitely sour. A wine waiter may only take a wine back if it is spoiled in some way, not just because you don't like it once it has been opened. A reputable wine store will also replace a corked wine if you return it (and the cork) promptly.

This wine is out of condition – again, use this phrase with caution in restaurants and wine stores. A white wine may be seen as 'out of condition' when it has turned deep gold (unless it should be this colour). It will taste like cheap sherry and caramel. A red wine which is out of condition will have a brown colour (again some old wine does go brown and is still drinkable, so be careful) and again will taste of caramel and not be pleasant to smell. Send it back, it will give you a headache if you do drink it.

Always remember that wine is a personal experience. No two people have the same taste buds and therefore a wine tastes different to each individual. So have confidence in your own point of view and express your feelings about a wine.

THE ART OF
WINE TASTING

Like any skill, wine tasting can be tackled at various levels. Everyone has heard of those legendary tasters who can identify the precise slope of the exact vineyard in a particular county in a wine-producing country. But these are rare birds – there may be only a dozen in the world and one of them is Michael Broadbent of Christie's, the auction house of London. He has written several authoratitive books on tasting and vintages which are readable but rather frightening for the amateur.

Why is it worth tasting wine at all? Surely it is easier just to drink it and not worry too much about the formalities of tasting. In a way this is true. Too much anxiety about tasting can detract from the simple enjoyment of wine. But at the same time a little knowledge gained from tasting adds immeasureably to the pleasure of the next drink with dinner.

There are four stages in tasting wine.

H O W   T O   T A S T E

APPEARANCE Consider first if the wine is clear and not cloudy or murky. Next, look at the colour. A young red wine will be purple, an older one tinged with brown. A typical fruity young white wine will be pale in colour like fresh hay or straw. A sweeter white wine takes on gold tints.

SMELL The next stage is to smell the wine. Smell is connected with taste so, in fact, the scent of the wine can tell you almost everything about it once you have mastered the techniques of smelling wine. One way to impress a wine waiter or your host is to swirl a wine in the glass, then scent it with your nose *without* tasting it. Nod approval in a subdued way once your nose has told you it smells agreeable. If for any reason it seems unpleasant then go ahead and taste to check that impression. But as a rule the nose is at least as important as the taste buds.

What is the smell of a good wine? In general, a good white wine will smell of the grape it is made from – or a blend of various grapes. This fresh quality often recalls a particular fruit or flower, depending on the grape varieties used. For instance, a Muscat wine really does have the fragrance of those grapes, which are also popular for eating. But a Riesling is far more flowery, like jasmine or elderflowers. A white wine from the Loire, such as **Vouvray**, smells of fresh peaches; a California **Colombard** may remind you of cantaloupe melon.

All these fruit or flower resemblances add up to one phrase for the wine taster – *aroma*. The aroma of a wine is quite simply the smell of the grape. It is highly desirable in most white wines which are made to be sold young (often within a year of making). Exceptions to the rule are certain white Burgundies such as **Montrachet** or **Meursault**, which have special characteristics due to being aged in wood.

The other element of the 'nose' is called *bouquet*. This is a more elaborate component that derives from the ageing process of the wine combined with the qualities lent to it by the skins of the grapes and the wood casks used to store the wine.

Bouquet is mainly an element of red wines. Apart from those white Burgundies and certain other wines such as white **Rioja** from Spain, white wines chiefly have aroma.

How to define a bouquet? As a rule, it is that touch of elegance and complexity in a wine which gives it style. Some French wine tasters, for instance, say that certain French Bordeaux wines remind them of the smell of expensive furs; or some say they have the suave scent of a cigar box, or of sandalwood. Old white Burgundies or vintage champagnes which are made with the same grape variety, Chardonnay (see the GRAPE GUIDE which follows) often smell like toast spread with rich fresh butter. So think expensive even when the wine isn't. Red **Rioja** from Spain need not cost a great deal, yet it often has a lovely smoothness and bouquet which smells of vanilla. This comes from the American oak casks which are used in its ageing.

Be creative in your comparisons for both aroma and bouquet.

Wine is like food or perfume, it has the whole range of appeal. A fine wine is like a fine gem or fragrance, it is crystal clear and true to itself. A lesser wine may have just as much charm but fewer lasting qualities.

TASTE After the nose the mouth plays its part. The taste of the wine should confirm its bouquet. If its aroma was fresh and fruity, it should taste slightly acidic. To detect acidity, think of lemon juice or a tart apple. If the taste of a white wine is sharp enough to make your mouth pucker, it could have too much acid, or an excess of one type called *malic acid*. With red wines, mouth puckering means *tannic acid*.

In time, the tannic taste mellows and becomes less harsh – the wine smooths out. The harsh qualities usually blend with the aromatic qualities of the young fruity wine.

Because there are few generally accepted words in English to describe taste, be creative when describing a wine. If it is not sweet, sour or bitter then you will have to think of a comparison with a familiar food or drink, or think of a garden comparison, or a reminder of the home (e.g. polished wood).

FINISH AND BALANCE These are the key words for the taster. *Finish* means the taste remaining in your mouth after drinking the wine – it may be lingering, limited or halfway between the two. Most everyday wines have very little finish, just as an everyday dress would not have couture seams or hand stitching.

A heavy, alcoholic wine will be rich and full-bodied. The taste of such a wine stays with you after tasting. Swirl the wine around your mouth as if it were mouthwash or gargle (seriously). A true taster would then spit out the wine before swallowing any. Any flavour that lingers is then the finish of the wine.

It is much harder to detect the finish of a more delicate wine such as a light German Riesling. What taste remains might be masked by food you have eaten or perhaps someone smoking nearby. For this reason, at a serious wine tasting nothing is eaten and nobody smokes. But do not despair. You will soon train your palate to detect a flavour. The real secret of tasting is to develop your memory. Use even unlikely comparisons to stimulate recall of a certain wine – does it smell like cooking cabbage, damp wool, or apple blossom? Let your imagination run riot for these memory joggers really do allow your skill as a taster to build. See the glossary overleaf for some more conventional terms commonly used to describe various wines.

The ideal wine is described as *balanced*. This term implies the 'right' combination of tannic acid, sweetness, fruity flavour and other characteristics for any wine. Most of all it means that the wine is true to itself, a quality hard to discern when you are learning to taste and you know few wines.

For example, the true style of a Mosel wine from Germany is fruity, yet light, low in alcohol, fresh and with plenty of acidity. A good Mosel will have all of these qualities, but none to excess – it will be balanced. An out-of-balance wine may have too much sugar, too much acidity, too much tannin, too much alcohol, or a combination of all of these.

WINE TASTING AT HOME

A wine tasting party is a good way to try many different wines. It is great fun and an efficient way to learn about the qualities of many wines. Invite a small group of friends – they don't have to be experts. Ask each to bring a bottle, such as a favourite wine or one they want to try for the first time.

Having a theme to the party is useful. You can try white wines from one region, red wines from another, or compare French and California wines.

Always taste from dry to sweet; try the youngest wines first, otherwise one wine may mask the flavour of the next. To make the party more exciting, try disguising the identity of the wines by wrapping each in a bag, or offering each wine by the glass without showing the bottle.

Evaluate each wine as you taste it and compare your impressions with those of your friends – then check with the label.

You need not spit out each sample after tasting, but don't try more than say, ten wines. Too much alcohol might impair your judgement! Each wine should be served in a stemmed glass and you need only a small quantity of each – at a professional tasting a typical bottle would serve about twenty people. Don't smoke or wear powerful perfume and serve some dry bread or plain crackers with water to rinse the mouth occasionally. Save that cheese for later – it makes even the cheapest red wine taste like nectar and masks its true style.

Wine tasting in a Spanish bodega

T A S T I N G
G L O S S A R Y

A guide to the vocabulary of tasting.

Aroma – this very important word has already been discussed. Remember that it is a description of the smell of the fresh grape and especially desirable in young white wines.

Baked – as the name suggests, a baked wine is make from grapes which have become very ripe or even begun to turn to raisins in a hot climate. In some areas this is a desirable quality for sweet wines such as the **Vin Santo** of Italy – such wine is made by drying grapes in the sun before they are pressed.

Big – a general term of appreciation for a full red or white wine, often quite alcoholic (say 13° or 14°/20% proof) with a 'mouth-filling' quality.

Blackcurrants – commonly associated with the Cabernet Sauvignon grape grown in France in Bordeaux and in California, Australia, South Africa and Chile. But other red grape types can also give a wine this flavour.

Body – an important term. A wine is either full-bodied, heavy or light. If it is a rich red wine but not full-bodied, then it might be described as 'out of balance'. Tasters describe the body of a wine when giving an overall assessment.

Bouquet – a term already discussed, associated with the ageing process of a wine. The bouquet of a wine is a complex smell which overlays the basic fresh aroma after time has passed.

Brick-red – the attractive russet tint of mature claret, **Rioja** or **Chianti**. The red of a very young wine is tinged with a little brown at the rim of the glass.

Brilliant – as the term suggests, a wine of crystal clarity. Most wine made today will have this quality.

Brown – with few exceptions such as old sweet sherry and Madeira, a wine should not be fully brown although it may have a brown tinge.

Clean – a term of approval meaning the wine has a fresh, straightforward attractive taste; often applied to white wine.

Cloudy – no wine should be clouded in the glass. If it is not transparent then there is something wrong with it, or the glass is dirty!

Complex – a favourite but irritating term of tasters which can mean many things. It is often applied to an aged red wine which has a range of flavour characteristics hard to pin down, such as claret, Burgundy, **California Cabernet Sauvignon**, or **Barolo** from Italy.

Corked – a wine which is corked has a mouldy cork and tastes of must and dampness.

Distinctive – a wine of character, a memorable wine with a particular and unusual taste.

Dry – wine without much 'residual sugar' (the sugar which remains in most wines after fermentation is complete).

Dumb – this wine needs to be 'aired' for a while before its flavour appears. It may be hard to smell anything on the 'nose'.

Earthy – commonly used to describe wines of Southern Europe. They have a pungent yet attractive quality which the French call the *gout de terroir* – the taste of their native earth.

Elegant – as the name suggests, a wine of style which is probably costly – it has no 'rough edges'.

Fat – a full-bodied wine, perhaps a little too heavy so it becomes unattractive.

Flowery – often used of the Riesling grape and other white grape types such as the Sylvaner and Gewürztraminer. The smell reminds you irresistibly of a flower in the garden.

Finish – the taste which stays with you after drinking or spitting out a wine. A finish may be long or short according to the wine but a 'lingering finish' is the sign of a fine wine.

Firm – a young red wine with plenty of flavour and tannin which will age well.

Flat – a dull wine with no memorable character.

Foxy – powerful smell of native American grapes such as the Concord, sweetish and spicy.

Fruity – as the name suggests, such a wine reminds you of certain fruits such as raspberries (Gamay) or blackcurrants (Pinot Noir).

Gun flint – some tasters claim the smell of gun flint can be found in certain very dry white wines such as the **Sancerre** and **Pouilly Fumé** of the Loire Valley (France).

Hard – a wine which needs time to mature and become smoother.

Lively – a wine with plenty of flavour but still young and fresh.

Maderized – A wine which has taken on a brown colour and caramel flavour showing that it is either too old to drink or it has been stored badly.

Noble – a wine made with one of the more famous grape varieties and a good example of its style.

Oaky – a wine which has too strong a flavour from the oak barrel.

Rough – a poor wine with a harsh taste.

Spicy – typical of the Gewürztraminer grape and a few other varieties, this aroma reminds you of the spices you use in the kitchen.

Stalky – if the grapes were not very ripe then they have a smell like grass and a slightly bitter taste – not good features in a wine.

Supple – a smooth agreeable wine.

Vanilla – an important term used in relation to flavour and given to red wines by oak ageing.

Yeasty – champagne smells pleasantly of yeast but other wines should not have too strong an aroma as it could mean the wine is re-fermenting in the bottle.

Rioja ageing in oak barrels

INTRODUCTION TO GRAPE VARIETIES

Grape varieties are fundamental to the understanding and appreciation of wine. First, a knowledge of these varieties will help you identify wines as many today are labelled according to grape type, notably certain wines from Australia, California, Italy (particularly the wines of North-East), Alsace and the wines of Eastern Europe (Hungary, Bulgaria, Yugoslavia). Secondly, the distinctive characteristic of many of these grape types contribute much to the end taste of the wine. A knowledge of the grape varieties will thus help the enjoyment of any particular bottle of wine.

There are many grape varieties to be found in the wine-producing regions of the world but the following are among the principal ones:

CABERNET SAUVIGNON
This grape is generally considered to be one of the two, if not the greatest, red wine grape of the world. Its classic home region is Bordeaux in France where it is regarded as a noble grape, but it has also been successfully transplanted to make fine red wines in, principally, California, Australia, South Africa and Chile. In Bordeaux, Cabernet Sauvignon gives claret or red Bordeaux its depth, its aroma, long-lasting flavour and keeping qualities. In the production of the classic red Bordeaux wines, Cabernet Sauvignon is normally combined with other Bordeaux grapes, chiefly Cabernet Franc and Merlot. In California the grape produces some of the region's finest red wines, notably from Napa and Sonoma. Experts say the grape can be recognised chiefly by its deep colour, the aroma almost of blackcurrants and by its fruity flavour.

CHARDONNAY
Another noble grape, Chardonnay, produces the great white burgundies of France and some of the finest varietal wines in California. It is also one of the three constituent grapes in French champagne. The wine it produces varies from a pale yellow such as **Chablis** to a deeper shade of yellow as seen in the Californian wines and white Burgundies such as **Meursault**. It is dry with a crisp bouquet and has a memorable fragrance at its best.

CHENIN BLANC
An important grape variety making dry to medium-sweet white wines in the Loire in France and in California, Australia and South Africa.

GAMAY
This is the grape of Beaujolais. It produces red wine in France and

California which is light in character and alcohol but with a striking, fruity bouquet and a distinctive pink-purple colour.

GEWÜRZTRAMINER
This aristocratic grape is well known in Germany, Austria, the Alsace region of France and California for producing a spicy, slightly scented, fragrant white wine. It varies in taste from fairly dry to medium-dry. Gewürztraminer is probably seen at its best in Alsace.

GRENACHE
A grape grown in the Southern Rhône and Midi in France, in California and in Australia. It produces a light, fruity red wine.

MERLOT
In both Bordeaux and California this grape is often blended with Cabernet Sauvignon to produce a more rounded red wine. It is the dominant grape in the famous wines of Pomerol such as **Château Pétrus** from the Bordeaux region of France.

PINOT NOIR
Generally considered to be one of the great red grapes of the world, it is seen probably at its best in the classic red wines of Burgundy such as those of the **Côte de Nuits** and **Côte de Beaune**. It has been less successful in other parts of the world such as California though some North American wine makers, particularly a number in Oregon, are trying to improve the flavour of wine made from this grape. Pinot Noir is also a constituent grape used in the making of French champagne. The grape has a distinctive aroma and is usually paler and with a subtler taste than Cabernet Sauvignon.

RIESLING
In many ways this noble grape is the white equivalent of Cabernet Sauvignon with a hardy, resilient character that it retains in the many regions of the world to which it has been transplanted. It is to be found probably at its best in Germany and Alsace (France) but the grape also makes fine wines in, among other places, California and Australia. Most Rieslings are dry to medium-dry but in Germany, in particular, some of the finest sweet desert wines are made from this grape.

SAUVIGNON BLANC
The grape is a constituent of the sweet white wines of **Barsac** and **Sauternes** in Bordeaux, France but also under the name of Blanc Fumé is the grape responsible for the fine dry wines of **Pouilly Fumé** and **Sancerre** in the Loire district in France. French wines called **Sauvignon** are often dry, light white wines. In California the grape and the wine produced from it can also be known as **Fumé Blanc**. The white wine produced from this grape has a spicy, distinctive flavour.

ZINFANDEL
This grape is uniquely Californian, producing mainly red, some rosé and of late, white wines and has a flavour usually described as 'berrylike'.

Merlot grape

READING THE LABEL

WINE LABELS

Building a clear understanding of how wine labels work is a key to learning about wine in general. There is much to be gained by a close study of a label. First, you are checking that the wine suits the occasion or purpose you had in mind. Second, you are able to judge something of the wine's quality by the details given about where it was made, bottled and shipped.

There is no doubt that wine labels can be very confusing. The use of traditional lettering or lengthy terminology on a label can mean that you are uncertain what it means. With luck, the colour of the wine will be apparent even through tinted glass, or the wine will be arranged by colour in the store, so that the first hurdle is overcome.

What to look for next? Start by seeing if you can identify the following information, which must be shown by law on all wines made and sold within the countries belonging to the EEC (European Economic Community) and other wine producing countries:

> quality of the wine as determined by EEC Regulations or local laws.
>
> country of origin of the wine
>
> name and address of the responsible bottler or brand owner
>
> quantity in the bottle or container (expressed in centilitres, or hundredths of a litre)

QUALITY INDICATOR

All wines actually made in EEC countries will give some indication of their quality status. In France, there is the *Appellation Contrôlée* for fine wines which limits production and guarantees a certain minimum quality. There is also a lesser category called *VDQS (Vin Délimité de Qualité Supérieur)* or a simple *Vin de Pays* for a local country wine of good standard. Other countries have similar systems.

QUALITY INDICATORS ON EUROPEAN LABELS

COUNTRY	TABLE WINE	'COUNTRY' WINE
FRANCE	Vin de table	Vin de pays
GERMANY	Tafelwein	Landwein
ITALY	Vino da tavola	Vino tipico

COUNTRY OF ORIGIN

This has to be the first thing to spot on the label. It is the initial clue to the style of wine you are examining. Look for the country title at the bottom of the label, usually expressed as **Produce of**.................
Almost all wine labels give some indication of where the wine comes from. However, within the EEC, wine described as table wine is frequently a blend of wines from more than one EEC country. It is labelled in the language of the country in which it is sold and the label often states that it is 'wine from different European countries'. German table wine, for example, contains large quantities of Italian wine.

NAME & ADDRESS OF BOTTLER / OWNER

It is important to decide if the wine is bottled and shipped by the company named and made elsewhere, or if it was made, bottled and sold direct from the producer. Most table wines are simply bottled and marketed after being made, perhaps using the facilities of a large winery or cooperative. But a finer wine will be controlled during production and sale by making, bottling and marketing direct. In Bordeaux, for instance, the wine will be labelled *mise en bouteilles au château,* and in Germany *Erzeuger Abfullung* if that wine is sold by the producer. See the label guide which follows for some more details.

The name and address given on the bottle are your guarantee for the wine. In theory, you could complain to those bottlers or shippers if the wine is not up to standard, but of course in practice you should return the wine to the store or wine merchant if it proves undrinkable for some reason.

Although frauds are occasionally detected in the wine trade, as a rule these labelling requirements prevent anyone passing off a poor wine as something better.

QUALITY WINES

AC or VDQS (e.g. *Appellation Médoc Contrôlée)*

QUALITÄTSWEIN (QbA) or QUALITÄTSWEIN mit PRADIKAT (QmP) with various levels from *Kabinett* through *Spätlese, Auslese, Beerenauslese to Trockenbeerenauslese* (drier to sweeter)

DENOMINAZIONE DI ORIGINE CONTROLLATA (DOC) or DENOMINAZIONE DI ORIGINE CONTROLLATA E GARANTITA (DOCG)

Château Moulis

750ml

12% vol.

MOULIS EN MEDOC

.1981.

APPELLATION MOULIS EN MÉDOC CONTROLÉE
J. DARRICARRÈRE, PROPRIÉTAIRE A MOULIS EN MÉDOC (GIRONDE)
MIS EN BOUTEILLES AU CHATEAU

PRODUCE OF FRANCE

QUANTITY IN THE BOTTLE

These days, your bottle may not even be bottle-shaped – it might be a box or a can of wine. But it will normally show the precise contents in centilitres.

The usual measures for a bottle of wine are either 70 or 75 cl., enough to serve about six standard glasses of wine. Beyond this is the litre, a popular favourite in Europe; then 1.5 litres, also known as a magnum (double bottle).

Other traditional European bottle sizes include, for champagne, the jeroboam (equivalent to 4 bottles), the rehoboam (6 bottles) and the methusalah (8 bottles). For claret, the double magnum contains the equivalent of 4 bottles, the jeroboam 6 bottles and the imperial 8 bottles. Many wines are also available in half-bottles but they are not usually good value for money since bottling and other overheads are the same as for a full bottle.

A modern container such as the wine box will hold anything from two litres upward and should be clearly marked. Remember that a case of standard-size wine bottles is nine litres, so compare cost and value when choosing one of these larger containers. Sometimes an inexpensive wine in bottles is as good value as the box and the wine may stay fresher longer.

OTHER OPTIONAL LABEL INFORMATION

Information which may also be found on a wine label could include the name of the **wine-making region**, in addition to the name and address of the shipper or producer.

The **vintage year** might also be mentioned, if the wine is of sufficient quality to merit a vintage date. A simple table wine or *vin de pays* style of wine has no vintage date. Nor do branded wines, as the aim with these is total consistency from bottle to bottle over the years.

You may find some indication whether the wine is **sweet**, **medium-dry** or **dry**, as well as some idea as to the **serving** temperature – 'served chilled' or *'servir frais'* on a white or sparkling wine.

Some wines have extra neck or back labels which may give **background on the winery**, the way the wine is made and the style of wine. The Californians and other US wines are especially helpful in this fashion.

A particular **grape variety** which predominates in the wine may be mentioned, usually below the name of the wine. This is common with German wines where you will see 'Riesling' or 'Sylvaner' below that lengthy wine title, and you can judge something of the style of the wine from the grape type.

Last but not least, the **alcohol content** of the wine may well be indicated. This can help your choice of wine, as you may well prefer a lighter wine (say 10°) with the first course then a heavier red wine (say 13°) with the main course. Remember that any wine of more than 15° is considered outside the table wine category and is usually a fortified wine.

OTHER USEFUL LABEL INFORMATION

AUSTRALIA & NEW ZEALAND: Both these countries give additional information on front and back labels, frequently including the grape variety or blend of grape varieties used.

ENGLAND: English wine is made from fresh grapes. There is also British wine which is made from imported grape *must* (concentrated juice).

FRANCE: *Blanc de blanc* is seen on some labels and means that the wine or champagne is made only from white grapes, and therefore is extra light. Claims such as *Grande Reserve* or *Cuvée Speciale* are meaningless under the law. *Supérieur* usually means that the wine is slightly higher in alcohol than the average for that region – it need not be higher quality.

GERMANY: *Trocken* means dry, and *halbtrocken* half-dry, in contrast to the usual style of German wine, which normally has a measure of sweetness. Sometimes German-looking labels are used for blends from other EEC countries, so do look for that country of origin indication.

ITALY: *Riserva* means that the wine has been aged for longer than the average. *Classico* means that the wine comes from prime sites within a particular region such as **Chianti Classico**.

PORTUGAL: *Verde* (as in **Vinho Verde**) literally means 'green' and indicates a young and fresh white wine. *Rosado* is a rosé, often slightly sparkling.

USA: Like Australia, copious information is frequently put on the back label – so don't forget to read it!

WINE LABELS
EXPLAINED

CÔTES DU ROUSSILLON

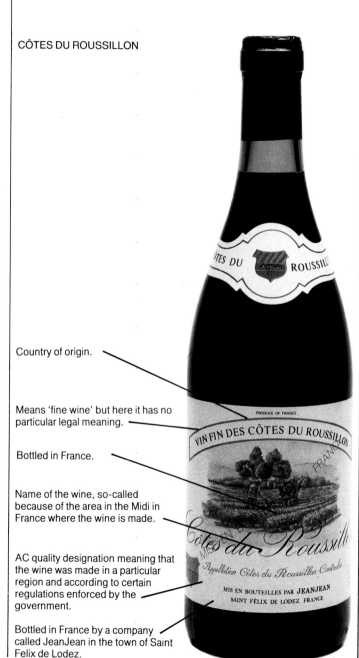

Country of origin.

Means 'fine wine' but here it has no particular legal meaning.

Bottled in France.

Name of the wine, so-called because of the area in the Midi in France where the wine is made.

AC quality designation meaning that the wine was made in a particular region and according to certain regulations enforced by the government.

Bottled in France by a company called JeanJean in the town of Saint Felix de Lodez.

LE PIAT D'OR

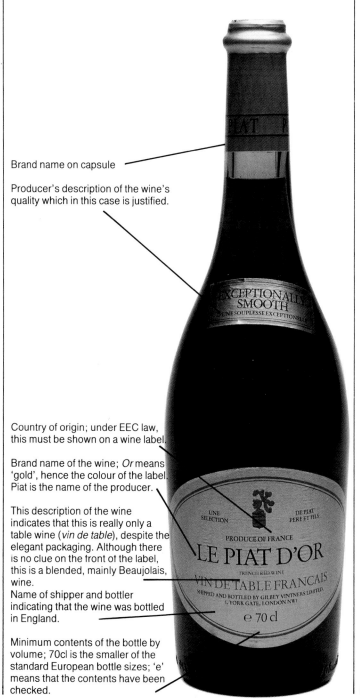

Brand name on capsule

Producer's description of the wine's quality which in this case is justified.

Country of origin; under EEC law, this must be shown on a wine label.

Brand name of the wine; *Or* means 'gold', hence the colour of the label. Piat is the name of the producer.

This description of the wine indicates that this is really only a table wine (*vin de table*), despite the elegant packaging. Although there is no clue on the front of the label, this is a blended, mainly Beaujolais, wine.

Name of shipper and bottler indicating that the wine was bottled in England.

Minimum contents of the bottle by volume; 70cl is the smaller of the standard European bottle sizes; 'e' means that the contents have been checked.

39

BROLIO CHIANTI CLASSICO

Name of the producer on capsule is extra guarantee.

Vintage date and producer's name; Chianti is good when young but will also keep for up to 10 years.

Brand name and type of wine: Brolio is one of the small number of independent estates producing Chianti Classico ('classico' indicates that the wine is made within a specific area in the Chianti region). It does not carry the black rooster (*gallo nero*) symbol because the producer is not a member of the Chianti Classico consortium to which over 90 per cent of this wine's producers belong. Brolio, incidentally, is the oldest Chianti Classico estate and claims to be the 'inventor' of Chianti.

DOC is a guarantee of reasonable quality and minimum standards being met. All Chianti Classico must have this quality designation or the higher DOCG status (generally for consortium Chianti Classico).

Bottled in the area of production (literally in the producer's winery at Gaiole).

Name and address/location of the wine producer – in this case Baron Ricasoli, Florence, Italy.

Minimum contents of the bottle by volume; in this case, 75cl, the larger of the standard European bottle sizes; 'e' means that the contents have been checked.

Percent of alcohol by volume; 12 per cent is fairly high.

BOLLA VALPOLICELLA

Signature of producer guarantees origin.

Vintage date. 1982 was a good year for this wine but it is not meant to be kept for more than five years.

Name of the producer. Bolla is a well-known wine company based in Verona.

Percent of alcohol by volume; 12 per cent is quite high.

Name of the wine, a light red wine made near Verona, Italy.

Minimum contents of bottle by volume. 700ml is equivalent to 70cl, the smaller of the standard European bottle sizes.

DOC quality designation meaning that the wine is produced in a specified area. In Italy, this means that it is superior to table wine (*vino da tavola*) but inferior to DOCG wine (certain wines from top-quality zones).

Classico indicates that the wine comes from the best area within its DOC region; *superiore* means that the wine is fairly high in alcohol (12 per cent in this case).

EEC definition of the wine; VQPRD (*Vini di Qualita Prodotti in Regione Delimitate*) is often found on labels of DOC wines and indicates that the wine comes from a specific area.

Bottled in Italy in the wine-producing area by, in this case, the producer.

Name and location of English shippers/distributors.

41

MOUTON-CADET

Owner of the estate; he oversees production and also controls marketing.

Vintage date; 1982 was a good year for basic Bordeaux wine.

Brand name of the wine. Literally 'junior Mouton', indicating that it is a cousin to the great wines made by the Rothschild family such as Château Mouton-Rothschild. It is one of the best-selling brands of superior blended Bordeaux wine.

AC quality designation, meaning that the wine was made within the Bordeaux region from particular grapes, according to certain specifications enforced by the government.

Owner's personal guarantee of the wine's quality.

Bottled by the owner in Pauillac, a famous wine village in the Médoc district of Bordeaux. *Négociants* means 'wine merchants'.

42

Country of origin indicated, in accordance with EEC regulations.

Name and address of British shippers.

Name of shipper. ——————

Country of origin; this must appear on the label under EEC regulations.

Crest of shipper. ——————

Name of the wine, so-called after the area of production. This is a dry red wine made within the Rhône area south of Lyon and north of Avignon. It is usually blended from various grape types and wines. *Côtes* means 'banks', in this case, of the river Rhône.

AC quality designation meaning that the wine was made in the Rhône valley and according to certain regulations enforced by the government.

'*Selectionné*' means 'chosen', indicating that the wine is probably blended, and bottled in France.

Bottler's address at Castillion-du-Gard in the south of France. The wine was probably transported there in tankers, then blended for export.

Minimum contents of bottle by volume; 70cl is the smaller of the two standard bottle sizes.

43

MARQUÉS DE RISCAL RIOJA

Seal attached by local authorities to guarantee minimum quality.

Traditional casing; some bottles are wrapped in sacking.

Minimum contents of bottle by volume; 75cl is the larger of the two European bottle sizes.

'e' means that the measure in the bottle has been checked.

Crest of the Marqués (Marquis) of Riscal.

Wine's producer; in this case, the 'heirs of the Marquis of Riscal'.

Area of production; in this case, in Elciego in the northern part (Alava) of the Rioja district of Spain. The district also gives its name to this wine.

Vintage date.

Rioja 'seal' identifies a genuine wine from the Rioja district in Spain.

Country of origin, a requirement on all wines produced in EEC countries.

Name and address of the bottler in Spain (in this instance, the producer).

Name and address of the British shipper.

Bodega (winery) established in 1860.

BELMONTE SOAVE

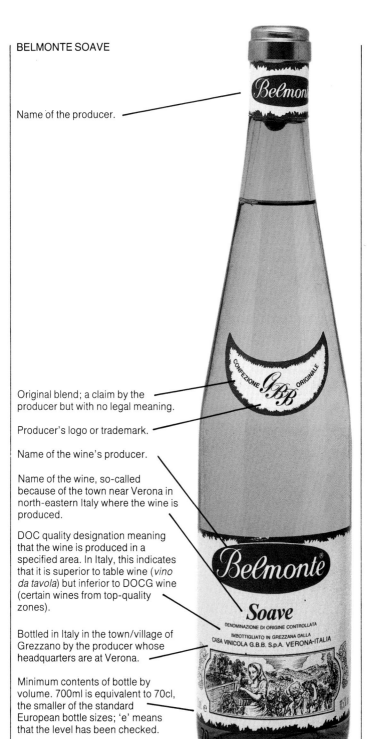

Name of the producer.

Original blend; a claim by the producer but with no legal meaning.

Producer's logo or trademark.

Name of the wine's producer.

Name of the wine, so-called because of the town near Verona in north-eastern Italy where the wine is produced.

DOC quality designation meaning that the wine is produced in a specified area. In Italy, this indicates that it is superior to table wine (*vino da tavola*) but inferior to DOCG wine (certain wines from top-quality zones).

Bottled in Italy in the town/village of Grezzano by the producer whose headquarters are at Verona.

Minimum contents of bottle by volume. 700ml is equivalent to 70cl, the smaller of the standard European bottle sizes; 'e' means that the level has been checked.

Percent of alcohol by volume. This is quite high for a white wine.

MUSCADET DE SÈVRE ET MAINE

Vintage date and type of wine; Muscadet should be drunk very young (under 3 years).

Producer's name.

Country of origin.

Serving advice; unusual to see this translated to English.

Name of the wine, called after the grape of the same name. Muscadet from the Sèvre and Maine area around Nantes in Brittany is acknowledged as the best of this wine. Muscadet without this area designation on the label is a simple wine of lesser quality. Should be a very dry, crisp white wine.

AC quality designation meaning that the wine was made according to certain regulations enforced by the government.

Bottled in the area of production – in this case in the Loire Valley at Saumur (up-river from Muscadet region).

Name and address of producer.

Minimum contents by volume

Percent of alcohol by volume; by law, the maximum alcohol content of AC Muscadet must not exceed 12°.

BLUE NUN

Name on capsule is a guarantee of authentic wine.

Brand name of the wine; *Blue Nun* is a trademark registered by Sichel, the producers and shippers.

Country of origin. This must appear on the label.

Abbreviation for H.Sichel Söhne (H.Sichel & Sons).

Brand name; *Blue Nun* is a major brand of Liebfraumilch, although not always the best value.

Wine may be bottled in UK since Sichel have offices in London as well as in Germany.

Quality designation meaning that the wine is of middle quality from the Rheinpfalz, one of the nine official wine districts in Germany. This designation often appears on labels as *Qualitätswein bestimmter Anbaugebiete (QbA)* – quality wines from specified wine-growing areas. This indicates that the wine is superior to table wine (*tafelwein*) but inferior to *Qualitätswein mit Prädikat (QmP)* – quality wines with special attributes.

Official quality number given after a sample has been tested and approved by the government. All *QbA* and *QmP* wines must have an AP number as a guarantee of quality.

Minimum contents of bottle by volume; 70cl is the smaller of two 'standard' bottles – the other is 75cl (¾ litre).

Vintage date and type of wine; Liebfraumilch is a blended 'soft' white wine which is medium-dry and of 'pleasant character'.

Name of the producer.

47

MÖET & CHANDON CHAMPAGNE

Capsule gives name of producer as a guarantee.

Literally 'first blend' but this has no legal meaning and refers to a non-vintage wine from Möet & Chandon, one of the biggest champagne houses. Almost all champagne is blended with great skill.

Möet & Chandon was founded in 1743 and their champagne was one of Napoleon's favourite drinks.

Name of the wine, so called after the small area east of Paris where the wine is produced. The word 'champagne' may only be used on wines made in the restricted Champagne area and by the *méthode champenoise*. In North America and Australia, however, the word is often used on domestically-produced sparkling wines.

One of the two major champagne towns; the other is Reims.

Minimum contents of bottle by volume; 75cl is a standard bottle size for champagne.

Country of origin; under EEC regulations this must appear on the label.

48

MATEUS ROSÉ

Produced, bottled and shipped by the producer.

Wine's producer. Sogrape is Portugal's largest winery, and Mateus rosé is the world's best-selling rosé.

Brand name of the wine.

Average capacity by volume. 700ml is equivalent to 70cl, the smaller of the two European bottle sizes; 'e' means that the level has been checked.

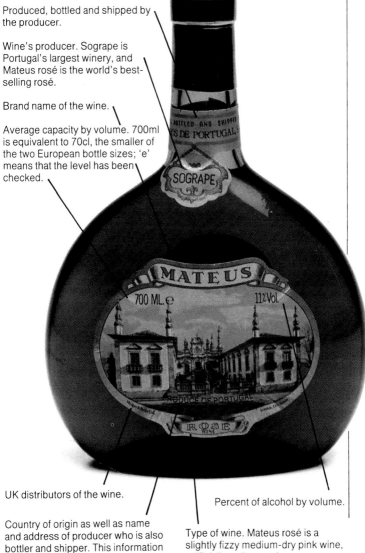

UK distributors of the wine.

Country of origin as well as name and address of producer who is also bottler and shipper. This information is repeated on the neck label.

Percent of alcohol by volume.

Type of wine. Mateus rosé is a slightly fizzy medium-dry pink wine, artificially carbonated.

THE CHOICE OF WINE

STYLES OF WINE

It is not enough to simply describe a wine as red or white, dry or sweet. Every wine you try is truly individual and this is why so much is written about wine and why so much mystique surrounds the subject. It is also one of the great attractions of wine.

In the next section WINES AND VINES you will find a handy reference to most of the names, grape varieties and descriptions that will be found on the wine shelves in your local store. This introduction will give you a head start on studying those shelves, but unless you grasp the essential differences between wine styles, you will not be able to pick out a bottle at all.

To help your selection, the whole repertoire of wines may be divided into three principal styles: LIGHT DRY WINE, SOFT AND FRUITY WINE, and RICH AND FULL WINE.

L I G H T   D R Y   W I N E

Here we have the wine of the moment. Light wines, under 13°, and often white, are very fashionable for several reasons. In our modern world, there is an emphasis on looking good and staying fit, and these wines can help to maintain that image.

If you drink only light wines of this kind in moderate amounts, you should not gain too much weight, providing you do not overeat, and they are unlikely to damage your health in any way. In fact, doctors have found that moderate wine drinkers are generally healthier than teetotallers, especially in statistics relating to coronary disease.

The problem with wine as a health drink is that opinions differ. French doctors, for instance, suggest that you need a full red wine rich in tannin to benefit your heart. This means you should concentrate on wines in the 'Rich and Full' category which follows.

Perhaps the answer is to get to know wines, then enjoy them in moderation. The first time you sample vintage port, for example, it could be tempting to take more than a glass or two. But the next morning your head will tell you that was a mistake. Vintage port is meant to be sipped very slowly and appreciated in small amounts, as are most fortified wines.

What is a moderate amount? Most doctors suggest that a man should drink no more than a typical bottle of wine per day – six average glasses making up 75 cl., or less than this of fortified wines. A woman (sadly) cannot absorb as much alcohol without risking liver damage in later life, so she should generally not exceed four glasses of wine a day. Naturally, having a good meal with your wine means the heady effect is diluted and, of course, wine is made to accompany food.

A light wine is ideal with a light meal or as an aperitif to sharpen your appetite before good food. It should be refreshing and have a 'clean' taste in your mouth, with some acidity. The effect of a good light wine is like drinking pure spring water or fresh fruit juice – delicate yet really refreshing.

There are red, white and rosé light wines. Some wines are actually promoted as 'light' wines in the US, meaning that they are low in calories, but this description does not fit only those few wines.

Any wine you might drink before a meal without feeling full after a glass or two is a light wine. It will be dry, and could have a very faint natural sparkle as in **Vinho Verde** from Portugal.

LIGHT AND DRY WINES OF THE WORLD

FRANCE: **Chablis, Muscadet, Alsace Riesling** and **Sylvaner**, Rhône rosé wine such as **Tavel**, white wines such as **Sancerre, Pouilly Fumé, Pouilly Fuissé**, Loire red wines such as **Sancerre Rouge**. Also most Bordeaux red wines traditionally known as **claret** are light and dry, although not the wines of St. Emilion or Pomerol.

GERMANY: All wines which are labelled *Trocken,* and Mosel wines up to *Kabinett* quality, also some wines from Baden. (Almost all exported German wine is white but if you find a red or rosé wine, it will normally be a light style).

ITALY: **Frascati, Soave** and **Verdicchio** white wines; **Valpolicella** red wine and certain **Chianti** which is not *riserva*.

SPAIN: **Rioja** white wines, white wines from Penedes (often made by Torres); **red Rioja** labelled *clarete*.

PORTUGAL: Any white wine labelled as a **Vinho Verde**; **Bucelas** white wine.

OTHER EUROPEAN COUNTRIES: **Fendant** white wines from Switzerland; all English wines whether red or white.

USA: **Fumé Blanc** from California; **Emerald Riesling** from California; white wines of the Pacific Northwest; **Aurora** white wines from Eastern States; **Delaware** white wines made from native US grapes.

AUSTRALIA: Some of the lighter **Rhine Riesling** white wines; some **Semillon** wines.

SOUTH AFRICA: Dry **Steen** wines.

SOFT AND FRUITY WINES

These are the wines which have appeal to the first-time wine buyer and drinker. They come close to a soft drink in style and provide a springboard from drinking only beer and Coke to experimentation with wine drinking.

Not all the wines in this category are mere 'fun' wines however. Some, like **Beaujolais** (**Gamay Beaujolais** in California) can lay claim to being among the world's fine wines – and certainly the Rieslings of Germany are the favourite of many wine connoisseurs.

Because they are so 'soft', and perhaps have a tendency to be sweet, these wines also make an ideal aperitif and may well accompany dessert if they are white wines. They have a particular appeal in summer or in hot climates as they are served cool and are delicious with light picnic food or barbecues.

The sweet aromas of grape varieties like Gamay, Riesling and Gewürztraminer recall summer gardens and the scent of flowers. Wine tasters use floral comparisons for wines which fall into this category – or sometimes soft fruits, like raspberries for the smell of Gamay or cantaloupe for the aroma of Colombard.

Fruity wines have charm and can be enjoyed at any time of day or night with equal pleasure. They are a safe choice for guests because their fruity aromas make each mouthful agreeable, but beware of serving them with food. Their floral scents can sometimes overpower your cooking. Serve them with full-flavoured dishes, such as fish soup or fried veal or chicken escalopes.

Wine lovers will enjoy the challenges of a 'hard' wine like Chablis or a complex wine like California Cabernet Sauvignon but these soft wines are their relaxation – a break from business, an escape from the real world.

Note that although tasters used the word 'fruity' to describe certain wines, they are still made from 100% fresh grapes. Any wine which is a blend of grapes and other fruits, or not made from grapes at all, may be a pleasant drink, but is not a real wine and is not discussed here. Who would need a 'semi-wine' when real wines offer such variety?

SOFT AND FRUITY WINES OF THE WORLD

FRANCE: **Vouvray** from the Loire (white); **Alsace Gewürztraminer**; **Beaujolais** (red); **Mâcon Blanc** and similar wines from Southern Burgundy; **Chinon** and **Bourgeuil** (red) from the Loire; **Anjou rosé**; lighter red Burgundies such as **Volnay** and **Santenay**.

GERMANY: Almost all German wines in the mid-price range fit this category. Well-known names like **Liebfraumilch** and **Niersteiner Gütes Domtal** are typical examples but most other names which are from the Rhine (including the Rheinpfalz and Rheinhessen) are safe selections. Any wine classified higher than *Kabinett* will be sweeter and richer.

ITALY: **Orvieto** (red or white); **Bardolino**, a light red; **Grignolino**; **Lambrusco** (usually slightly fizzy red); any white wine named as made with the Trebbiano or Pinot Grigio grape varieties.

SPAIN: **Red Rioja** of less than *reserva* quality; red wines from Penedes of less than *reserva* quality.

PORTUGAL: **Mateus rosé**; other Portuguese rosé such as **Lancers**.

OTHER EUROPEAN COUNTRIES: Yugoslavian Riesling such as **Lutomer**; light white Austrian wines such as **Schluck**; **Dôle** red wine from Switzerland.

USA: **Riesling** and **Grey Riesling** white wines of California; **Gamay** from California; **Chenin Blanc** and **Colombard** from California; most California rosé. **Riesling** and **Gewürztraminer** of the Pacific North West. New York wines made with the Chelois (red), Cayuga (white) and Seyval Blanc (white) and most rosé of this region.

AUSTRALIA: **Rhine Riesling** and **Trebbiano** white wines; also **Riesling** from New Zealand.

SOUTH AFRICA: **Chenin Blanc** and **Colombard** white wines.

R I C H   A N D   F U L L   W I N E S

Although the previous two categories have their fair share of fine wines, including claret and Chablis for example, the majority of the world's 'great' wines are described as rich and full. In our grandparents' day, the most popular quality wines were all sweet – **Sauternes, Barsac, Tokay, Rhine wines.** Now taste has moved toward the drier wines, yet many of the world's great wines are still heavy and rich in flavour without sweetness.

This category breaks down into two classes: rich, powerful wines which are not sweet, many of which are red, and truly sweet and rich wines, most of which are white.

A 'full-bodied' wine is likely to be fairly high in alcohol – perhaps between 12° and 14°. It will have a depth of flavour which comes from ageing, often in wood, even for white wines, and will continue to improve over many years. The legendary white **Tokay** wines of Hungary have been known to survive for over a century and still be drinkable. Even today a good **Sauternes** will have keeping qualities which mean it can be enjoyed after 30 years or more. The relatively high alcohol combined with the sugar content acts as a preservative.

Drier wines such as red **Burgundy** or fine Italian wines like **Barolo** have a long life expectancy also. Modern winemaking techniques have led to the production of many traditionally full red wines in a somewhat lighter style (**Rioja** is a good example, but the 'heavyweights' are still available. In Burgundy, try a **Pommard**; in the Rhône, a **Hermitage;** in Italy, a **Brunello di Montalcino**.

The interesting fact about full wines is that winemakers thoroughly enjoy making them. They demand great skill and care, and give great rewards to the wine lover, but patience is required. Virtually none of the wines in the following lists may be consumed young – under three years old – and most benefit from about ten years of maturity. Serve these wines with full-flavoured dishes, with strong cheese, or with really ripe fruits if the wine is a sweet one. This type of wine is definitely meant to accompany food and shows its best virtues with a well-made meal.

RICH AND FULL DRY WINES OF THE WORLD

FRANCE: **Pomerol** and **St. Emilion** from Bordeaux; red **Burgundies;** white Burgundies such as **Montrachet** and **Meursault** but not nearby Chablis or Mâcon Blanc (light and fruity respectively); all red Rhône wines and most white wines of this region (e.g. white **Hermitage**); red wines of Provence; red wines of the South West (e.g. **Côtes de Roussillon**).

GERMANY: Most of the fuller German wines are sweet. The only exception is Franconian wine, also known as **Steinwein** after the shape of the bottle. It is full, dry and white.

ITALY: *Amarone* versions of **Valpolicella** are very rich and full; **Barolo** and **Barbaresco** from Piedmont; **Brunello di Montalcino** and **Vino Nobile di Montepulciano** from Tuscany; **Chianti** labelled *riserva;* **Spanna** and **Gattinara** from Piedmont.

SPAIN: Red **Rioja** wines of *reserva* quality; **Gran Coronas** and similar wines from Penedes.

PORTUGAL: **Dão** red and white wines.

OTHER EUROPEAN COUNTRIES: **Bull's Blood** and similar red wines from Hungary; Bulgarian **Cabernet Sauvignon**; most Yugoslav red wines; Greek red wines such as **Othello**; Israeli wines (not Kosher wines, as these are sweet).

USA: **Cabernet Sauvignon, Petite Syrah, Zinfandel** and **Barbera** of California; **California Chardonnay** and most **Riesling;** New York wines made with the Baco Noir or Foch grape varieties.

AUSTRALIA: **Cabernet Sauvignon, Shiraz** red wines; some **Semillon** white wines.

SOUTH AFRICA: **Pinotage, Cabernet Sauvignon** red wines; many good red blended wines such as **Roodeberg.**

RICH AND FULL SWEET WINES OF THE WORLD

FRANCE: **Sauternes** and **Barsac** from the Bordeaux region; Côteaux du Layon from the Loire Valley; *vendange tardive* (late harvest) wines from Alsace; various **Muscat** wines from the South of France including **Muscat de Beaumes de Venise; Monbazillac** from the Bergerac area.

GERMANY: All wines labelled *spätlese, auslese, beerenauslese* or *trockenbeerenauslese* will be sweet in increasing degrees and the price will rise with each grade of sweetness – do not expect a *spätlese* to be very sweet, however, except in a great vintage such as 1976.

ITALY: **Est!Est!Est!** from near Rome is semi-sweet; **Lacryma Christi** from Naples; some **Orvieto; Vin Santo** from Tuscany (made with dried grapes); **Picolit,** a rare speciality white wine.

SPAIN: Best known for fortified wines, as is PORTUGAL.

OTHER EUROPEAN COUNTRIES: **Tokay** from Hungary, although today it is rarely as rich as it was in the 19th century (the sweetest is **Eszencia);** white wines of Austria labelled as are German sweet wines, and often less expensive; **Commanderia** from Cyprus made with dried grapes; Greek **Mavrodaphne,** an unusual sweet red wine, also sweet white wines made with Malvasia and Samos muscat grapes; various red and white Israeli wines.

USA: Late harvest red and white wines of California made with varieties such as Riesling, Gewürztraminer, and even Zinfandel; other California white wines made with Malvasia and muscat; Concord red and white wines of New York; also wines made with the old Niagara variety.

AUSTRALIA: German-style sweet white wines; other dessert wines made with Semillon and other varieties.

SOUTH AFRICA: Like Australia, best known for sweet fortified wines, but has some dessert white wines such as the **Edelkeur.**

S P A R K L I N G   W I N E S

There is a sparkling wine to fit each category already mentioned.
Champagne, for instance, starts its life completely dry after it has
been fermented twice (the second fermentation takes place in the
bottle you eventually buy) – yet is rarely sold this way.

As a general rule, a sparkling wine is not as dry as, say, a Chablis,
because it tastes rather harsh and indigestible. If you want to
sample such a wine for yourself, look out for the occasional bottle
labelled *natur* or 'no residual sugar'. Sadly there is no way that we
can pretend that sparkling wine is a diet aid, but in a way it does help
your health – it is good for the digestion and also lifts your mood
rapidly due to the action of those bubbles on your stomach lining.

Remember that the word *sec* or its equivalent applied to the
sparkling wine does not mean it is completely dry. Confusingly, the
word *brut* on a bottle of champagne often denotes a drier wine than
one labelled 'extra dry'.

So study your labels carefully and seek advice. There are a few
general rules, such as knowing that **Asti Spumante** from Italy is
always quite sweet, and German sparklers are normally fruitier than
the French equivalent. The following list may guide your choice.

Drier sparklers: Champagne labelled *brut;* sparkling wines from
Burgundy which may also be titled *brut* or *sec;* Spanish sparkling
wines made by the *méthode champenoise* also labelled *brut;*
California 'Champagne' (which may not carry that name in the EEC)
also indicating *brut* or 'dry'.

Fruity sparklers: German **Sekt,** made by the proper method and
from the Riesling grape; most Italian sparkling wines apart from Asti
Spumante; sparkling wines of the Loire Valley such as sparkling
Saumur; sparkling red **Burgundy;** less expensive California
sparkling wine often made with the Chenin Blanc grape; Australian
sparkling wine; New York State 'champagne'.

Rich drier sparklers: Vintage-dated real champagne; superior
Spanish *cava* sparkling wines; top California 'champagne' eg.
Schramsberg, Korbel.

Rich sweet sparklers: Champagne labelled 'rich' or *doux;* other
French sparkling wine so titled; **Asti Spumante;** muscat sparkling
wines from California.

F O R T I F I E D   W I N E S

Again these range over the wine spectrum. Although they are
higher in alcohol than table wine, this does not mean that they are
necessarily sweet; many drinkers make this mistake after an early
introduction to a sweeter style of fortified wine, perhaps **amontillado**
sherry in the UK or **angelica** in the US.

The refreshing almost 'salty' flavour of a **manzanilla** sherry from

Spain can be a shock to the palate yet this is a true fortified wine (in its country of origin it is not always fortified however – the brandy is added for export). At the other extreme, try a **Malmsey** Madeira or an old-fashioned brown sherry for mouth-filling sweetness.

Each of the major fortified wines appears under various guises. See below for a guide to styles but remember not to be misled by previous experience into selecting, say, a bottle of port for someone who likes a very rich sweet wine. You may find it is *white* port which is served crisp and cold as an aperitif, or even mixed with tonic or soda in its native Portugal.

The most important use for a fortified wine is after a meal, but the dry styles are equally happy as before-lunch or dinner drinks. With the move today away from lengthy, rich meals the producers of these traditional wines are urging us to try them over ice, in long drinks, on picnics, anywhere. Experiment for yourself and do not let tradition inhibit your style.

Dry fortified: *Fino* and *manzanilla* sherry; dry **montilla**; sercial, verdelho and rainwater **Madeira**; **dry vermouth** sometimes known as 'French' vermouth, also occasionally flavoured with additional herbs as in the fragrant Chambery style; **white port.**

Fruity fortified: *Amontillado* sherry; **marsala** (without the egg); **Malaga** from Spain; **ponche** from Spain and Portugal; **angelica** from the US; *rosé* and *bianco* **vermouth**; ruby port.

Rich and dry fortified: Dry *oloroso* sherry; old **madeira**; vintage and old **tawny port.**

Rich sweet fortified: pale or dark **cream sherry**; Italian sweet vermouth; Bual and **Malmsey** Madeira; marsala all uovo; muscatel from Setubal in Portugal, from France, or from the US; **tawny port** less than five years old.

WHAT'S IN A BOTTLE

A GUIDE TO THE PACKAGING OF WINES

Much advertising today seems to suggest that the wine bottle we know may soon be redundant. 'The first bad year for the bottle' says one US advertisement for wine which is sold in cartons like fruit juice, and many others advertise the superiority of wine in cans or in special boxes which have taps for serving.

Why is wine usually offered in a glass bottle anyway? Why should it have a cork – why not a screw cap or crown cap like a beer bottle? Why are there rules about wine 'packaging' which have waited this long to be broken? The answers are mixed.

First, wine has benfited from modern technology like any beverage or food product. New ideas are intended to make wine easier to present in stores, easier to keep at home and easier to

serve. It is all a part of the wine-drinking revolution which is making wine as easy to drink as beer, and as informal.

Because wine is subject to chemical change even after it has been made and bottled, many experts have puzzled how best to retain its freshness. For white wines this is vital as their charm is in the light fruity quality of a young wine. Certain preservatives are permitted, such as sulphur, but best of all is to avoid letting the wine linger long on the shelf before sale. Alternatively, the wine may be treated so that it no longer tends to age or change in the container – something like pasteurization.

This type of process is frowned upon by the purist. For the wine buff, wine must be allowed to 'breathe' and to age over the years as it always has, by an exchange of air through the cork in the bottle or through the wood cask.

The problem with this is that many people do not want an aged or particularly subtle wine – just something easy and agreeable to drink. For them, the convenience of the package, whether a box or a can, is all important. So the new packaging is unlikely to go away, nor is the traditional bottle which is the best medium for 'fine' wines.

THE BOTTLE

Made of glass which is commonly tinted to keep out the light, this will have a cork or screw cap with a foil or plastic 'capsule' over the neck. If it has a cork you will of course need to find a corkscrew. The cork allows air in gradually over time and this 'smooths' the wine but it can also allow the wine to rot. Typical bottle sizes include 70 or 75

cl., one litre, 1.5 litres and 2 litres, as well as certain traditional European sizes mentioned on page 00.

THE BOX
Made of cardboard but lined with a plastic 'balloon', this has a tap with a valve which prevents air getting into the wine. The balloon gradually collapses as the wine is consumed. The system was pioneered in Australia and the French, for instance, resisted this idea for a long time, then borrowed Australian technology. Americans have also developed this idea. Sometimes the wine in the box does get too much air and becomes flat or 'tired', but a box is a good notion for parties and barbecues or for people with limited storage space. Wines offered in boxes are generally not top quality, but may well be varietals (see WINES AND VINES) and well-made. Usual sizes: 3 litres, 6 litres, 9 litres or variants.

THE BRICK
Also known as a TetraPak, this type of package suffers by looking too much like fruit juice – you snip off the corner and decant into a jug or straight into glasses. Of course, like fruit juice the freshness is lost once you have opened the pack, but since it is not a very large quantity this should not matter. Some tasters say they can detect the taste of cardboard in the wine. Usual size – half or one litre.

THE CAN
A simple aluminium can as used for soft drinks which chills readily and holds enough for one person at a picnic or outdoor event. As with the brick, tasters claim to detect a metallic flavour in the wine, but as a rule it is very faint. Small measures like this are also sometimes offered in 'mini bottles' or mini cartons. Fruity wines like **Beaujolais** keep well in cans.

What next for the wine industry? The Japanese have pioneered the use of crystals – dehydrated wine – but as yet have not dried anything really worth drinking. With 'six packs' of wine already a reality, there is no excuse not to pick up as much or as little wine as you need at any time, but the cork is unlikely to disappear. Synthetic corks may catch on, but at the moment it is still the cork oak which helps to give the better wines their distinctive flavour.

UNUSUAL BOTTLES
Certain wines have striking traditional containers, or fantasy 'jugs' such as those invented for the everyday wines of California. These, like labels, can be amusing to collect. First on many lists would be the flask-shaped bottles used for **Mateus rosé** and for the **Steinwein** of Germany (Frankenwein). Then there are the 'crocks' – bottles which look like stoneware – holding Portuguese wine or German **Liebfraumilch**. Some Italian wines, notably **Chianti**, come in curious twisted bottles which may have long necks – hand-made and expensive. And there is the *fiasco* – that straw-covered flask which today is rarely seen due to its high cost of manufacture.

Larger bottles have handles to aid pouring, or may be shaped like a carafe for ready transfer to the table.

Of course you can learn to recognise the basic bottle shapes quite quickly and know what is being served before you see the label.

THE HOME
WINE CELLAR

This need not be a true cellar as long as it is cool and dark without undue vibration. The temperature should not rise above 21°C (70°F). Arrange your wines in racks in a fairly logical sequence if possible. Keep any fine wines for ageing farthest from the door and young, everyday wines nearby.

Make your selection from the categories above. A good basic selection of two dozen bottles (two cases) would consist of:

4 bottles dry white wine
4 bottles fruity white wine
4 bottles dry red wine
4 bottles fruity red wine
3 bottles rich full red wine

2 bottles rich sweet white wine
1 bottle dry fortified wine
1 bottle sweet fortified wine
1 bottle sparkling wine

Adapt this according to your taste but try to replace stock as it is used up. Then you will never be caught unawares by a guest who wants 'something sweet' or who requests a dry red wine before dinner. Humour them, then recork the bottle and keep it in the refrigerator, or put back in a cool cellar. Use the unfinished bottle within five days and nothing is wasted. If all else fails, that spare wine will certainly improve your menus for a few days, and you will have shown yourself a generous and thoughtful host or hostess.

WINES & VINES

Mountainside vineyards in
the Alto Adige region of Italy

WINE-PRODUCING
REGIONS
OF THE WORLD

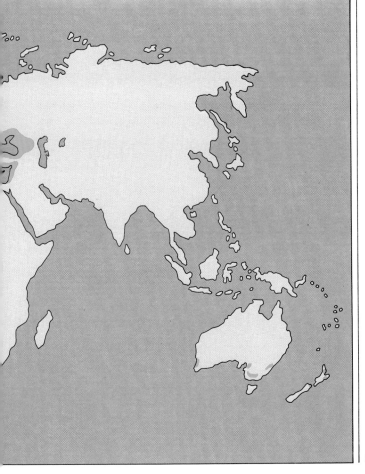

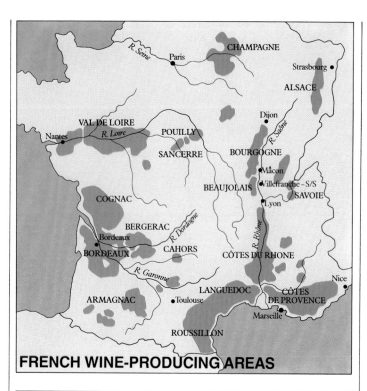

FRENCH WINE-PRODUCING AREAS

GERMAN WINE-PRODUCING AREAS

ITALIAN WINE-PRODUCING AREAS

US WINE-PRODUCING AREAS

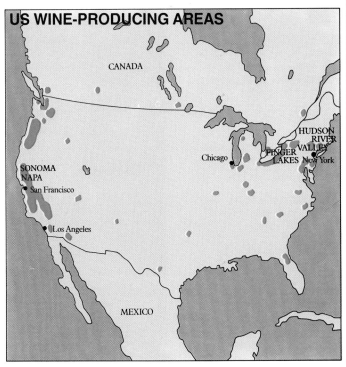

WINE
DICTIONARY

In this section you will find the information you are likely to need about the wines regularly available in stores and restaurants. The dictionary lists not only names of wines, but also wine terms such as 'dry' and names of grape types and familiar branded wines such as **Mateus Rosé**. Use the listings for quick reference at home or when you are out to dinner – and get to know your wines better.

A

ABBOCCATO Italian description of 'medium-dry' wine.

ABRUZZI Italian wine region producing wines from the montepulciano (red) and trebbiano (white) grape varieties.

AC See *Appellation Contrôlée*.

ACIDITY An essential aspect of wine's flavour giving balance and crispness.

AHR German wine region south of Bonn best known for red wines which are rarely exported.

ALAMEDA County in San Francisco Bay area where Concannon, Wente and Weibel wineries are located.

ALBA Major wine centre of the Piemonte (Piedmont) in Italy.

ALICANTE BOUSCHET Deep-coloured red wine grape of California's Central Valley – best known winery making a varietal wine with this is Papagni.

ALGERIA Formerly an important supplier of wines for blending purposes to France, today is independent and rarely exports. However wines are quite well made, especially the reds.

ALIGOTÉ Grape producing tart acidic white wines of the same

name in the Burgundy region of France – ideal for mixing with *crème de cassis* to make Kir.

ALMADEN One of the largest US wineries with a high proportion of production in jug wines.

ALOXE CORTON Well-known Burgundy wine town in the Côte de Beaune area. Best wine is simply **Corton** (red) and best white wine is **Corton Charlemagne.**

ALSACE Important though small wine region on the borders of France with Germany along the Rhine river. Wines are usually varietally labelled (by grape type) and include excellent fruity whites such as **Riesling, Sylvaner, Gewürztraminer** and **Muscat.** Sweeter wines are made by picking late and are called Late Harvest. (See also *vendage tardive*). Red wines are made with Pinot Noir but are rarely sold abroad.

ALTO ADIGE Mountainous region in northern Italy – part of the Trentino area for wine production. Here wines are made with Cabernet and Merlot

Vineyards in Alsace, France

(red) and Riesling and Gewürztraminer (white). Exports include red wines labelled **Santa Maddelena** and **Caldaro**.

ALTO DOURO Correct name for the region where port is made in Portugal by the river Douro. Each estate is called a *quinta,* then the various ports are shipped down river or by truck to Oporto for blending and ageing before shipment.

AMARONE Literally 'bitter' in Italian. Also particular method of making Italian red wine, especially **Valpolicella** – some grapes are left to dry on racks after picking which makes the wine much richer – although not sweet (a sweet red wine like this is called *Recioto*).

AMONTILLADO Medium-dry sherry usually dark in colour with a 'nutty' flavour.

AMTLICHE PRÜFUNGSNUMMER (AP) On German wine labels, the official quality testing number. All *QbA* and *QmP* wines must have this number which guarantees that they have been checked for quality.

ANBAUGEBIET Name for an official German wine region such as the Rheingau – there are 11 in all. A quality wine from a named region is known as QbA *(Qualitätswein bestimmter Anbaugebiete).*

ANJOU A province of the Loire best known for its rosé, which may be dry or semi-sweet, pleasant dry white wines made with the Chenin Blanc grape such as **Saumur** (which is a good name for sparkling wines also), and rich sweet wines including **Quarts de Chaume**

and **Coteaux du Layon**.

APPELLATION CÔNTROLÉE French quality designation. French wine law defines certain regions and wine types which may claim this special, superior status. These wines are regulated by a government agency. The legislation is designed to protect the consumer and the producer from imitations. Wines made under these rules must be produced from particular grapes, pruned in a certain way, and sold at a minimum strength and quality. The words *appellation côntrolée* have to appear on the label of an appropriate bottle.

APULIA District of Italy best known for production of large quantities of vermouth and some other wines including those sold under the San Severo label which have a DOC status.

ARBOIS Town in the Jura mountains in France where wines are produced, including unusual dry white wines made by drying grapes before fermentation – best known is **Château Chalon**. These wines are known as *vin jaune* or *vin de paille* (straw). There are also good rosés made here and some pale red wines which are not often exported.

ARGENTINA A major wine producer which does not export in quantity to the US or Britain at present. Their red wines are better than their whites and are varietally labelled as in California. Look for **Cabernet Sauvignon** or **Merlot**.

AROMA The smell of the grape found in all good wines, especially when young. Very desirable in white wines.

AMADOR County in the Sierra east of Sacramento in USA growing good Zinfandel.

ASTI Town in northern Italy where the famous sparkling wine called **Asti Spumante** is made – sweet and fragrant from the muscat grapes used. Asti is also the home of the Italian Swiss Colony winery in California.

ASZU A very sweet grade of **Tokay**, made in good years.

AUDE Vast wine area in southern France making table wines and some quality wines such as **Corbières** and **Minervois** which have the designation VDQS *(Vin Délimité de Qualité Supérieur)*. These are smooth agreeable red wines at good prices.

AUSLESE A German wine which is of top quality and also made from late-picked grapes so that it is quite sweet – sweeter than **Spätlese**, less sweet than **Beerenauslese** – and generally quite expensive.

AUSONE, CHÂTEAU Renowned property in St.

AUSTRALIA Increasingly important wine-producing area with good climatic conditions for reliable red and white wines as well as sparkling and fortified wines. The major regions are South Australia around Adelaide; the Hunter Valley north of Sydney (which produces wines with a slight 'volcanic' taste); and Victoria. Most wines for export are labelled varietally as in California with **Cabernet Sauvignon** and **Shiraz** notable for full red wines and **Rhine Riesling** and **Semillon** for white wines. Wineries here, as in California are of two kinds; either the small specialist 'boutiques' or the large-scale producers. A great deal of Australian wine is sold in the new wine boxes or by the 'cask' (a plastic container). This reflects the outdoor lifestyle of Australia. Well-known larger producers include **Seppelt** (who make 'Great Western' sparkling wine); **Thomas Hardy**; **Henscke; Kaiser Stuhl; Penfold's**; and **Lindeman** whose **Ben Ean Moselle** is one of Australia's top-selling wines. Renowned smaller producers include **Château Tahbilk, Rothbury Estate, Lake's Folly** and **Hickinbotham**.

Tollana vineyards in Barossa Valley, South Australia

Emilion, Bordeaux where one of the two top red wines of this area is produced mainly from the Merlot grape variety – rare and special.

AUSTRIA Wine is produced around the city of Vienna and much is consumed locally and during the festival of the *heurige* when the new wine is sampled fresh from the cask. The white wines are exported and these resemble German wines. They are often less expensive and graded similarly by sweetness – look for **Rhine Riesling** and **Grüner Veltliner** varieties. One brand to watch for is **Schluck**, a reliable blended wine. The top name from Vienna is probably **Gumpoldskirchner.**

AUXEY DURESSES One of the wine towns of Burgundy in France making fairly light red wines which may offer good value.

B

BACO Types of vine grown in the eastern US. They are hybrids, a cross between American and European varieties and resist frost well. Baco noir is best known, and is often blended with other varieties for added smoothness.

BADEN German wine region which produces reliable everyday wines rather than great wines. It is located in the scenic Black Forest in southern Germany. Most of its wines are made in a giant cooperative at Breisach. The top wines are made in the Kaiserstuhl area from the Rulander grape (white), called Pinot Gris in France. The region also yields a good rosé

called **Weissherbst** and some light red wines including **Affenthaler.**

BANDOL Major wine of Provence in France made in the beautiful Riviera. Rosé is best but white and red are also produced.

BANYULS A fortified wine made in the south of France and served as an aperitif in many French restaurants – very rich and sweet.

BARBARESCO Red wine of Piedmont in Italy similar to **Barolo** and considered among Italy's best. It needs to breathe before drinking. Made from the Nebbiolo grape.

BARBERA Another full red wine from Piedmont which is also successfully produced in California, notably by the Sebastiani winery.

BARDOLINO Delicate red wine made at Lake Garda in Italy. It should be served cool and when very young and fresh. Made from a blend of local grapes.

BAROLO A classic Italian wine from Piedmont which needs to air for at least three hours before drinking and can live for decades. It is made from the Nebbiolo grape, like Barbaresco.

BARSAC Second only to **Sauternes** as the major name for French sweet wines affected by the so-called 'noble-rot' or *botrytis*. These rich golden wines are dry on the finish and make a lovely end to a meal. Names to watch for include **Château Coutet** and **Château Climens.**

BEAUJOLAIS A triumph of

marketing, this fruity red wine is famous as *nouveau* or *primeur* – the young wine shipped only months after it is made. It is best served cool; refrigerate for a couple of hours then allow to warm slightly before serving. This wine is made from the Gamay grape which has a distinctive raspberry scent. There are nine important Beaujolais villages which make the best and longer-lasting wines: **Brouilly**, **Côte de Brouilly**, **Chénas**, **Chiroubles**, **Fleurie**, **Juliénas**, **Morgon**, **Moulin-à-Vent**, and **St. Amour**. Other simpler wines are sometimes called **Beaujolais** or **Beaujolais Supérieur** and are made in various other villages in the region. Most is drunk while under three years old. There is a little white Beaujolais produced but this is not usually exported.

BEAUMES DE VENISE Home to a fine sweet French wine called **Muscat de Beaumes de Venise**. This dessert wine is full with a subtle, lingering flavour. This district in the southern Rhône also produces a good dry red wine.

BEAUNE This beautiful and ancient city is a centre for the wines of Burgundy, many of which are blended or bottled here. An annual auction, which is called the *Hospices de Beaune*, sets the prices for the coming season. Wines simply labelled **Beaune** are made in the immediate area and some may be titled *Premier Cru* (first growth).

BEERENAUSLESE A *beerenauslese* wine is made with hand-selected grapes affected by the *Edelfäule* or 'noble rot', like Sauternes. Such wines are rare and very expensive and do not go with food – they are meant to be sipped with reverence.

BERGERAC A neighbour of Bordeaux in France, making similar wines which are usually very good value. Their pride is **Monbazillac**, a sweet white wine, but most people prefer the dry white (made with the Sauvignon grape) or red (made with the Cabernet grape).

BERNKASTEL Important German wine town in the Mosel region. Wine is made with the Riesling grape and is typically crisp and light with plenty of fruit.

BINGEN Town in the German Rheinhessen area which produces soft fragrant white wines from the Riesling grape.

BLANC DE BLANCS Any white wine made from only white grapes (remember almost all grape juice is white regardless of grape colour). This phrase is seen most often on fine champagne which is made from Chardonnay grapes and is especially delicate and consequently expensive (e.g. **Taittinger Comtes de Champagne**). However there are many dry still white wines to be found in France and California to which this description is applied.

BLANC DE NOIRS White wines produced from black grapes only – seen on champagne and in California for still wine.

BLANC FUMÉ A name for the wines of Pouilly in the Loire region of France and for wines made with the same grape in California (the Sauvignon Blanc). These white wines are very dry and clean-tasting.

BLANQUETTE DE LIMOUX An inexpensive sparkling wine from the Midi region in France. It is dry and made by a version of the *méthode champenoise.*

BOCKSBEUTEL The traditional flagon of Franconia in Germany similar to the Mateus Rosé bottle – used for the Stein wines.

meaning wine cellar or winery.

BODY Tasting term referring to the feeling of weight a wine has in the mouth, connected with the alcohol content.

BONNES MARES Famous red Burgundy with typical full rich flavour.

BORDEAUX One of the world's great wine regions in France producing a number of fine wines, both red and white. The reds are commonly known as **claret** in Britain. The whites may be dry or very special sweet dessert wines such as **Sauternes**. One third of French wine exported to the US comes from this large region. The major areas are: the Médoc, with the villages of **St. Estèphe, Pauillac, St. Julien** and **Margaux** producing magnificent red wines from the Cabernet Sauvignon and Merlot grape types; **St. Emilion** and **Pomerol**, also home to fine red wines; Bourg and Blaye, which have less expensive red wines; **Fronsac**; and **Premières Côtes de Bordeaux. Graves** makes fine dry red and white wines, and to the south is the **Sauternes** area yielding rare

| **BODEGA** Spanish word

Digging the soil, part of vineyard maintenance, Bordeaux, France
Below: Newly-picked grapes at a wine cooperative, Bordeaux

sweet white wines from the Sauvignon Blanc and Semillon varieties. **Entre Deux Mers** is a large area which is a source of very pleasant inexpensive dry white wines. The best wines are château-bottled to ensure quality.

BOTRYTIS CINEREA The botanical name for the mould which affects certain grapes and concentrates the juice – thus producing sweet rich wines such as **Sauternes, Beerenauslese** and **Trockenbeerenauslese** wines.

BOUQUET The complex scent of a wine which has been aged in wood and well made.

BOURGEOIS Means 'middle class' in French and is applied to certain Bordeaux wines which are not in the top classification but still very good.

BOURGOGNE Means 'Burgundy' in French. Wines carrying this name may be from any part of the region and are probably blended.

BOURGUEIL Town in the Loire region of France which produces fine red wines from the Cabernet Franc grape – fruity and with a nutty tang.

BOUZY Believe it or not, the name of a village in the Champagne region of France where light red wine is made – some goes to tint pink champagne and a very little is marketed.

BRIX The unit used by American wine makers to measure with a hydrometer the sugar content of grapes.

BROUILLY One of the principal nine Beaujolais wine villages

making good fruity red wines – light and agreeable when young.

BRUNELLO DI MONTALCINO Top red wine of Italy from Tuscany; very rich in flavour and prized by connoisseurs.

BRUT French term for dry wine; used in champagne, remember that Extra Dry is actually sweeter than *brut*. *Brut* champagne is available as a vintage or non-vintage wine and the description has been borrowed by other countries such as Spain for their sparkling wines.

BUAL Sweet Madeira served as a dessert wine – fortified.

BULGARIA Today a major region although before the 1950s very little wine was made here. Best is the full and powerful red **Cabernet Sauvignon** (wines are labelled varietally) and the white **Chardonnay**. Bulgarian wines are good value for money if you like your wine strong and straightforward.

BURGUNDY A much-borrowed wine name which should really only refer to those wines made in a particular region of France. Burgundies are distinguished by their richness and smoothness, whether red or white. The central area for winemaking is called the Côte d'Or (gold slope) and is centred on Beaune. North of there is the home of the fine red wines on the so-called Côte de Nuits (name taken from the town of Nuits St. Georges). The lower portion of the Côte d'Or is called the Côte de Beaune and is renowned for white wines.

The major grape varieties grown here are the Pinot Noir for red wines and the Chardonnay for white wines.

No 013553

Bourgogne 1979
Hautes Côtes de Beaune

APPELLATION CONTROLÉE

Ce vin, sélectionné en 1984 par les Jurés-Gourmets de la

Confrérie des Chevaliers du Tastevin ®

a été élevé et mis en bouteille par

Les Caves des Hautes Côtes

GROUPEMENT DE PROPRIÉTAIRES-RÉCOLTANTS - ROUTE DE POMMARD A BEAUNE (COTE-D'OR)

75 cl

FILIBER A NUITS

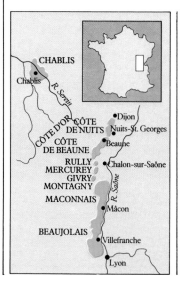

These varieties are also planted south of the Côte d'Or in an area called the Chalonnais that includes the areas of **Rully** and **Mercurey** which offer good wine value. Further south is the Mâconnais, home to **Mâcon Blanc** as well as **Pouilly Fuissé**, a popular delicate white wine.

The name Burgundy is also used elsewhere as a generic term to describe certain wines in, for example, California.

79

Cabernet Sauvignon grape

C

CABERNET The calling card of two notable grape types; the Cabernet Sauvignon and Cabernet Franc. Both are grown in the Bordeaux region of France where the Sauvignon is seen as the noble grape, long-lived and full, while the Cabernet Franc is lighter and fresher. Sauvignon is very successful in other parts of the world such as Bulgaria, California and Australia. While Cabernet Franc is not as widely planted, it does yield pleasant wines in the Bergerac and Loire regions of France. Cabernet grapes may be used for red wines or rosé.

CAHORS Heavy dark wine made in central France, high in alcohol.

CALIFORNIA Producer of the vast majority of US wine (over 80 per cent), this region has a fabulous climate and plenty of modern know-how to make reliable everyday wine as well as fine wines. Principal areas include the Napa and Sonoma valleys to the north of San Francisco where many of the best-known top wines are made including **Beaulieu, Freemark Abbey, Mondavi, Sebastiani** etc. South of the city are the **Santa Clara** vineyards around San Jose including **Almaden** and **Paul Masson**. In the hotter Central Valley are found many giant wineries including **Gallo, Guild** and **United Vintners**.

Every style of wine is made, from very dry whites such as the **Fumé Blanc,** to medium whites including the legendary **Chardonnay,** light reds such as **Gamay,** full reds including **Cabernet Sauvignon** and

Zinfandel, as well as dessert wines and fortified wines such as **Ficklin port**. Champagne-style wines are very well made here and are available in every price range – one of the finest is **Schramsberg**. Paul Masson, for instance, makes excellent sparkling wines at reasonable prices.

CANADA An adverse climate has meant an uphill struggle for the Canadian wine industry. Most wine is made around Lakes Erie and Ontario from native American grape types as well as hybrids like the Chelois, but in Ontario and British Columbia there are now some plantings of European varieties such as the Chardonnay.

CANTENAC Neighbouring village to Margaux in Bordeaux region of France and home to fine clarets such as **Château Palmer**, **Château Brane-Cantenac** and **Château Prieuré-Lichine**.

CANTINA Italian for 'winery'. A *cantina sociale* is a cooperative of winegrowers.

CAPSULE The seal over the neck of a bottle, made of lead, aluminium or plastic.

CARIGNAN Common red grape type in the south of France and North Africa used for table wines. Also planted in California and called Carignane.

CASE Wooden box or carton holding twelve standard bottles (about 9 litres of wine).

CASK Wood barrel used for ageing wines, particularly red wines. Casks vary in size, but as a general rule the smaller the cask the finer the wine because the woody flavour is more pervading.

CASSIS Means 'blackcurrant' in French. These are made into a liqueur which is mixed with dry white wine to make a **Kir** aperitif. Cassis is also a town in the south of France where various wines are made, notably white wines.

CASTELLI DI JESI Wine area in central Italy where light dry white **Verdicchio** wine is made.

CATAWBA Native American grape type used for wine and grape juice in eastern US – also for sparkling wines.

CAVE Means 'cellar' in French. *Visitez nos caves* means 'visit our wine cellars'.

CAVIT Stands for *Cantina Viticultori*, major cooperative near Trento in Italy, producing large quantities of table wine.

CHABLIS A much abused wine name used for all types of white wine worldwide. The real thing is produced in very small amounts in a little area to the north of Burgundy in France. A typical Chablis is bone dry and very light and subtle, made with the Chardonnay grape. Wines simply labelled **Chablis** or **Petit Chablis** are the regular styles. There are also *Grand Cru* wines such as **Vaudesir**, and *Premier Cru* wines (one step down) including **Montée de Tonnerre** and **Fourchaume**. All real Chablis is likely to be expensive because of the limited production. The wine name is used generically in California and Australia.

CHAI French overground cellar where wine is made and stored, particularly in the Bordeaux region.

81

CHAMBERTIN Famous red Burgundy with surrounding important names such as **Clos-de-Bèze** and **Charmes-Chambertin**. Pricey but the essence of red Burgundy.

CHAMBOLLE-MUSIGNY A Burgundy town where fine red wines are made, including the fine **Musigny**. **Bonnes-Mares** is another notable name here. The wines are made from the Pinot Noir grape.

CHAMPAGNE A name randomly applied to many of the world's sparkling wines, but, strictly speaking, a fine wine made in the province called Champagne in northern France. The champagne method (or *méthode champenoise*) is slow and expensive but yields wines of exceptional quality and flavour. Most champagne is white but some rosé is made by adding a local red wine called Bouzy.

Famous champagne houses include **Moët & Chandon, Taittinger, Bollinger, Veuve Clicquot** and **Pol Roger**. All make a basic house style and a vintage wine in good years, as well as a deluxe brand for special occasions, such as **Dom Pérignon** from Moët & Chandon. Champagne may be very dry *(brut)* or very sweet (rich) but a little sweetening is always added to the basic very dry sparkling wine before shipment.

CHARBONO Red wine grape grown in California similar to the Barbera.

CHARDONNAY A famous white wine grape grown worldwide, yielding wines which have a distinctive buttery flavour. Some are very light such as **Chablis**, others very rich such as fine **white Burgundies** and **California**

Checking champagne corks for splits or imperfections, Champagne, France

Chardonnay. The Chardonnay vine does not give a big crop, but it gives high quality. It is sometimes called the Pinot Chardonnay.

CHARMAT Name of a bulk process used in the making of sparkling wines – the fizz is added in giant tanks by a second fermentation. These wines are usually good value for money.

CHASSELAS White grape used for **Pouilly-sur-Loire** in France (not for **Pouilly Fumé**) and called Gutedel in Germany and

Mont-Redon, one of the best-known Châteauneuf-du-Pape wine estates in the Rhône Valley, France

Fendant in Switzerland.

CHÂTEAU The finest French wines of Bordeaux are described as château-bottled, i.e. bottled on a particular estate. Not all châteaux are very grand and some are simple country homes. Think of the phrase as meaning estate-bottled rather than implying some special superiority.

CHÂTEAUNEUF-DU-PAPE A red full wine from the French Rhône Valley made from a blend of some 13 grape varieties including the Syrah and the Grenache. These wines tend to be high in alcohol (up to 15°/ 20% proof) and long-lived. The name means 'pope's castle' because the summer home of the mediaeval French Pope was in the nearby town of Avignon.

CHENAS One of the nine named Beaujolais villages in France. See also *Beaujolais*.

83

CHENIN BLANC Widespread white grape variety originating from France's Loire Valley where it yields **Vouvray** and **Quarts de Chaume** among other wines. It also does well in California and in South Africa (as the Steen grape).

CHEVAL-BLANC, CHÂTEAU Best known top red wine of St. Emilion made with mainly the Merlot grape and of outstanding quality in almost any vintage.

CHIANTI Very popular wine from Tuscany in Italy once sold in picturesque flasks covered with raffia, but today in Bordeaux-style bottles. Almost all is red and made chiefly from the Sangiovese grape. Many have a very slight 'prickle' which results from a secondary fermentation in the bottle. **Chianti Classico** wines are made in a particular area between Florence and Siena and most have a seal with the symbol of a rooster. Another consortium is called **Chianti Putto** (cherub). **Chianti Riserva** (aged for at least 3 years) frequently has the bouquet of a wine aged in oak.

Vineyards and wine estate in the Chianti district of Tuscany, Italy

• •

CHILE Large wine producer (second-ranked in South America) with an excellent climate and French winemakers. Best wines are made with Cabernet Sauvignon or Barbera grapes (red), and Riesling (white). The white wines are shipped in flat flasks like Portuguese rosé and all the wines are of good quality and very low in price. Some of the best-known producers to watch for include **Concha y Toro**, highly rated for their Cabernet Sauvignon wines; **Cousiño Macul**, one of the oldest vineyards; **San Pedro**; and **Undurraga**, which exports to the USA and Europe – their wines include **Cabernet**, **Riesling** and **Pinot Noir**. One interesting point about Chilean vines is that they were never attacked by the bug *phylloxera*, which destroyed Europe's vineyards in the 19th century, so no grafting of vines is necessary as in Europe.

CHINON Town in France by the river Loire which produces a fine red wine from the Cabernet Franc grape. A favourite of the writer Rabelais centuries ago and should be drunk young.

CHIROUBLES One of the nine named Beaujolais villages.

CLARET Term used to describe the light red wines of Bordeaux, borrowed by other countries for their red wines made with Cabernet or similar grapes. (e.g.

clarete in Spain).

CLASSICO In Italy this designation indicates the wine is from a specific area within a region defined by the producers themselves, such as **Chianti Classico, Soave Classico.**

CLASSED GROWTH In France, one of the châteaux which was listed in the official Classification of 1855 (Médoc and Sauternes) and 1955 (St. Emilion) as a top estate. Only one change has occurred in the Médoc list since 1855. **Château Mouton-Rothschild** was promoted to first rank joining **Château Latour**, **Château Lafite**, **Château Margaux** and **Château Haut-Brion** (in the Graves district). Some properties now produce little or are less important, while others have improved over the years, for instance, **Château Lynch-Bages** or **Château Batailley**.

CLOS French for an enclosed vineyard such as **Clos de Vougeot** in Burgundy. The enclosed site once meant better quality grapes and wine although today some *clos* are no longer enclosed by a wall.

COMPLEX A taster's term for an interesting wine with plenty of 'nose' and difficult to define — subtle.

COLOMBARD Grape originating in the Cognac region of France where its wines are distilled for liqueur. In California and South Africa Colombard is used to make pleasant fruity wine and is the backbone of many blends and branded wines.

CONCORD Famous American native variety used in grape jams and jellies as well as wine. The wine is normally sweet and has a distinctive pungent taste often described as 'foxy'. Concord grapes are used in kosher wine and in sparkling **Cold Duck** (blend of red and white wines).

CONDRIEU Rare white wine from the Viognier grape made in the Rhône Valley.

CONSORZIO Group of producers in a quality Italian wine region, such as *Consorzio Vino Chianti Classico*.

COOPERATIVE In France cooperatives are common arrangements whereby growers make individual wines then sell them to the coop for treatments and bottling as well as marketing.

CORBIÈRES Source of good value red wines in southern France labelled as VDQS. Fitou is the best local wine and is of AC status.

Vineyards in the Corbières district in the Midi, France

CORNAS Red wine from the Rhône valley in France made with Syrah grape.

CORSICA Part of France, this island produces undistinguished wines in the Italian style – rarely exported.

CORVO Red and white wines of Sicily – agreeable but not of DOC.

COSECHA Spanish term for date or vintage that often appears on the label of Spanish wines.

CÔTE Means 'slope' in French. Throughout the world the best vineyards are on south or west-facing slopes.

CÔTE DE BEAUNE With the Côte de Nuits, this is one half of the legendary Côte d'Or (gold slope) in Burgundy producing magnificent red and white wines. Some have village or vineyard names such as **Montrachet, Pommard**. Others are named after the entire *côte* and are quality blends, produced by local shippers.

CÔTE DE BROUILLY One of the nine named Beaujolais villages.

CÔTE DE NUITS In Burgundy, France, the wine-growing area in the northern half of the Côte d'Or centred around the town of Nuits-St-Georges. Major vineyards include the fabulously expensive wines made at the **Romanée-Conti** small estate. Wines labelled **Vosne-Romanée** are named from the local village and are often reasonable value for plenty of flavour.

CÔTE RÔTIE Superior French red wine made in the Rhône

Vineyards in the Côtes de Provence
France

Vineyards of Chapoutier,
Côtes du Rhône, France

Valley. *Rôtie* means 'roasted' and the climate is hot here so the wine is full and spicy, and will keep well.

CÔTEAU DU LAYON Sweet white wine made in the Loire Valley in France from Chenin Blanc grapes affected by botrytis, the noble rot. Top names within the area are **Bonnezeaux** and Quarts de Chaume.

CÔTES DE PROVENCE Wines from the sunny south of France, well known to vacationers including a good rosé, often sold in unusual shaped bottles, and the white wines of Cassis and the red wines of Bandol.

COTEAUX DU LAYON Sweet white wine made in the Loire list, these are chiefly red wines made along the Rhône Valley in France – if the wine is called **Côtes du Rhône** it may be a blend from anywhere in the region, but it may also have an individual village name if superior, such as **Vacqueyras** or **Lirac**. These red wines have a spicy rich flavour as do the local white wines. The rosés are orange coloured and highly regarded by connoisseurs.

CRÉMANT Name for a special type of Champagne which is not fully sparkling – regarded as

special by the producers, particularly a **Crémant de Cramant** (named for a Champagne village). *Crémant* is also used to designate other sparkling wines of the world with the same meaning.

CRÉPY Wine from the Savoy region on the borders of France and Switzerland – slightly fizzy and very refreshing white wine for skiiers.

CROZES-HERMITAGE Notable village in the Rhône Valley in France where the famous red wine called **Hermitage** is made, as well as a white wine of the same name, and lighter wines under the village name.

CRU French term for a quality wine such as *premier cru* 'first growth'. If classified as in Bordeaux, they speak of a *cru classé*.

CUVÉE French word describing a blend – the contents of a vat. If the bottle is marked *grande cuvée* it means the producer is proud of that wine, but the phrase has no specific legal meaning.

CYPRUS Island in the Mediterranean which has made wine for centuries and still produces sound red, white and rosé wines as well as 'sherry' (popular in Britain) and a rare dessert wine called **Commanderia.**

D

DÃO Name of a Portuguese region producing red and white wines. The red is very fine with a slightly harsh quality when young, but very powerful and good when older (five years or more). Good value.

DECANTING The process of transferring wine from the bottle to a carafe or similar container.

DEIDESHEIM Top town in the Rheinpfalz for good soft white wines made with Riesling. Look for those made by Dr. Burklin Wolf.

DELAWARE A native American grape type used for grape juice and sparkling wines, as well as table wine.

DEMIJOHN Glass container which substitutes for a wood cask when storing wines – some wines are sold in these large 'bottles' which may be half covered in raffia and contain up to 10 gallons.

DEMI-SEC Literally means 'medium dry' but a champagne with this label will be sweet.

DENOMINAZIONE DI ORIGINE CONTROLLATA This is the Italian equivalent of the French *Appellation Controlée* and is applied to a wide variety of wines which are of good quality. There is also a higher grade called *DOC e Garantita* (DOCG) which is for a very few top wines only. The DOC laws have existed since 1963 and this abbreviation on the label is a useful quality guide, although relatively few non-DOC wines are sent to Britain or the US.

DENOMINACION DE ORIGEN Spanish equivalent of the French **Appellation Controlée** although such a designation does not always guarantee great quality.

DESSERT WINE A vague term often used in the US to refer to fortified wines as well as some naturally sweet table wines.

DOC Abbreviation for *Denominazione di Origine Controllata*.

DÔLE Swiss red wine made with Gamay and Pinot Noir grapes.

DOMAINE French word for a wine estate.

DOUX Means 'sweet' in French; used for the sweetest champagne.

DRY Simply the opposite of sweet – all (or almost all) the grape sugar has turned into alcohol.

DUBONNET Well known French fortified wine, served as an aperitif, which is sold as a red sweet style or white medium-dry similar to vermouth.

DURKHEIM Wine town in the German Rheinpfalz region, producing red and white wines – only the whites are exported.

E

EARTHY Taster's term for a wine which has a pronounced flavour and is quite heavy. Many Rhône wines have this flavour as do some Australian red wines and California wines from the Central Valley.

Frozen grapes used to produce *eiswein* in Germany

ECHÉZEAUX One of the wines made near the legendary vineyard of the Romanée-Conti in Burgundy – a fine red wine from the Pinot Noir grape – rare and expensive.

EDELFÄULE German term for 'noble rot' – the grape condition which produces the great sweet German wines.

EISWEIN German wine made with grapes that have literally frozen on the vine late in the harvest season. The result is added sweetness and flavour. If picked on Christmas Eve, the wine is called **Christwein**.

ELTVILLE Wine town in the Rheingau, one of the major wine regions of Germany.

EMERALD RIESLING Hybrid grape produced by the scientists at the University of California at Davis. Paul Masson makes the most popular wine from this grape – it has a fragrant yet clean flavour.

EMILIA ROMAGNA Italian wine region where **Lambrusco** semi-sparkling red wine is made and other red and white wines.

• •

ENGLAND The English wine industry is in its infancy but has begun to make an impression in the wine world, with light dry acidic white wines made with grape varieties including the Müller-Thurgau of Germany (a cross between Riesling and Sylvaner) and the Seyval Blanc of France (another hybrid vine). Two good recent vintages in 1983 and 1984 mean English wine is now fairly widely available, although tax rules mean it is fairly expensive compared with some European equivalents. Names to look for include **Hambledon; Adgestone** and **Barton Manor** from the Isle of Wight; **Felstar** form the East Coast; and **Westbury** from Berkshire.

93

ENTRE DEUX MERS Part of the Bordeaux region in France where mainly dry white wine is made as well as some pleasant red wine labelled **Bordeaux** or **Bordeaux Supérieur**.

ERBACH German wine town in the Rheingau region including the famed Marcobrunn vineyard. **Erbacher Marcobrunn** is a well-known example.

ERZEUGERABFÜLLUNG Means that the wine has been bottled in Germany by the producer.

ESPUMOSO Spanish term to describe sparkling element in certain wines.

ESTATE BOTTLED As a rule, an estate-bottled wine is of good quality because the producer has bothered to make, treat and bottle the wine in one place to ensure it stays in perfect condition. In France this usually appears on the label as *Mise en bouteilles au château* (Bordeaux) or *Mise en bouteilles au domaine* (Burgundy). In Germany it is *Erzeugerabfüllung*.

EST!EST!EST! A medium-dry white wine made with Trebbiano and Malvasia grapes near Rome, Italy.

ESTUFA Process used in **Madeira** to heat wines. It is intended to reproduce the effects of the original method which was to send the wine on a long hot ocean voyage. This gives the characteristic 'baked' flavour.

ETNA Italian wines made on the slopes of this Sicilian volcano – reasonable quality with DOC status.

F

FENDANT Swiss grape type, called Chasselas in France.

FERMENTATION The chemical action of yeasts on grape sugars to make wine.

FILTRATION Technical term for clarifying a wine by passing it through a filter, always done before bottling.

FINGER LAKES Wine region in New York State named after four lakes. Major wineries include Taylor, Pleasant Valley and Gold Seal.

FINING Technical term for clearing a wine of particles by adding an agent such as dried blood, egg white or special 'earth'. Used in conjunction with filtering.

FINO A very pale dry sherry from Spain.

FIXIN Red Burgundy from the north of the Cote d'Or in France.

FLEURIE One of the nine named Beaujolais villages in France for good red wines.

FLORA White hybrid grape variety grown in California.

FOLLE-BLANCHE White grape type used to make wines which are distilled into Cognac. Also grown in the Armagnac district in France and in California.

FORST Important wine town in the Rheinpfalz region of Germany (also known as the Palatinate).

FORTIFIED WINE A wine to which grape brandy is added to stop the fermentation and raise the alcohol level. Examples are sherry or port.

FRANKEN German province not far from Frankfurt which is source of fine, dry, so-called **stein** wine bottled in distinctive flasks called *Bocksbeutels*. The centre is Wurzburg.

FRASCATI Very popular and inexpensive Italian dry white wine made near Rome. There is also a medium-dry version.

FRECCIAROSSA Italian branded wine made as red, white and rosé in Lombardy – medium quality.

FRIULI-VENEZIA GUILIA

Italian wine region near Austria which makes wine mainly for domestic consumption although some of the rare sweet wine called **Picolit** is exported.

FRIZZANTE Italian term (meaning 'slightly fizzy') for those wines which have a little sparkle from a seondary fermentation. They are not true sparkling wines. An example is **Lambrusco**.

FRONSAC Minor area of Bordeaux in France that produces a reliable dry red wine – good value.

FURMINT Hungarian grape variety grown in the area where **Tokay** is made.

FURST German word for 'Prince' as in **Furst von Metternich**.

G

GAILLAC Obscure region of southwest France making semi-sweet white and sparkling wines.

GAMAY Important red grape variety tasting of raspberries which is made into **Beaujolais** and some good Loire wine in France, as well as pleasant California wines.

GATTINARA Italian red wine made in Piedmont – very rich and full. Needs ageing and time to breathe before drinking.

GEISENHEIM The German town where wine research is carried out and some good Rhine wines are made. Part of the Rheingau. Noted for **Riesling** white wines.

95

GENERIC A quality wine described simply by its region of production e.g. Bordeaux. Outside the EEC, however, it may be a wine of no specific origin but which is of a particular style, such as **Claret** (meaning the wine is of a light dry red style). Today this type of labelling, including **Chablis** and **Burgundy**, is falling from favour in the US and is illegal in the EEC because it is confusing and harmful to producers of the 'real thing'. An alternative is to use simply **Red Wine** or **White Wine**.

GERMANY Very important wine country for all types of wine, but mainly top quality white wine which is 'off dry'. Some German wines are sold as brands such as **Blue Nun**, which is a **Liebfraumilch**. The finest have a village name, such as Piesport, which is added to the vineyard name, Goldtropfchen, to make **Piesporter Goldtropfchen**. Wine making in Germany is tough because of the cold climate and winemakers are allowed to add some sugar to the juice before fermenting to bring up sugar levels and ensure adequate alcohol. As mentioned elsewhere, the three quality levels in Germany are *Tafelwein* (including *Landwein*), *QbA,* and *QmP* (see page 34). This last category includes wines at varying sweetness levels namely *Kabinett, Spätlese, Auslese, Beerenauslese, Trockenbeerenauslese.* There are 11 major German wine regions such as Rheingau or Mosel, all listed individually in this directory. As a rule, Rhine wines are bottled in brown glass, Mosel wines in green glass.

GEVREY-CHAMBERTIN Important wine town in Burgundy in France which produces a good quantity of red wine under the town name as well as the exceptional wine labelled **Chambertin** and various others with the Chambertin attached to the vineyard name, such as **Charmes-Chambertin**.

GEWÜRZTRAMINER Spicy and distinctive white grape type grown in the Alsace region of France where it makes fruity, dry wines, and in Germany and Austria for medium-dry or sweet wines. This grape also does well in California.

GIGONDAS Wine area in the Rhône Valley in France which makes good rich red wines and some fine rosé. Not far from the renowned **Châteauneuf-du-Pape** – good value.

GRAF German for 'count' – some noblemen own vineyards.

GRAND CRU A French term for a superior wine from a classified vineyard – in Burgundy and Chablis these are the very best wines. In Bordeaux, a *grand cru* is not necessarily as good as a *cru classé.* In St. Emilion there are many *grand crus,* but only 11 *premier grand crus.* Some of the *grand* are not very exciting wines. In Alsace they produce *grand cru* wines made with named grape varieities. In Champagne, *grand cru* on a label means the wine is made from grapes grown in a particular village which has vines worth more than a neighbour because of their reliable quality.

GRAVES This district of Bordeaux in France begins in the outskirts of the city. The name means 'gravel', which is desirable for growing wine grapes because it means the soil is well drained. Fine red and

Stony soil in the Graves area of Bordeaux, France

white wines are made here. Once the white wines were mainly sweet, but today demand has led to more dry versions – usually clean and crisp. The most famous red Graves is **Château Haut-Brion**, a first growth in the 1855 Médoc classification. Other notables include **Château Bouscaut**, **Château Carbonnieux**, **Domaine de Chevalier** and **Château la Mission-Haut-Brion**. The red wines of Graves are very smooth and have an exclusive and expensive aroma some tasters liken to that of a mink coat.

GREECE One of the first places on earth where wine was made and still a major wine producer, although a large quantity is made as **retsina** –flavoured with resin to give a curious tang which is not to everyone's taste but goes well with Greek food cooked in olive oil. Other notable wines are the sweet red **Mavrodaphne**, the dry red **Othello** and **Demestica**, and the sweet white muscat of **Samos**, made from late harvest grapes. Wines are also made on many of the Greek islands including Crete and Santorin.

GREEN HUNGARIAN White grape type grown in California which is mainly used for blending.

GRENACHE One of the red grapes which go into fine Rhône wines such as **Châteauneuf-du-Pape** and to make the orange-tinted, full-flavoured rosé of **Tavel** and **Lirac** in the same area. It is important in the making of Spanish red **Rioja** and also thrives in California.

GREY RIESLING Grape which produces light delicate white wines in California, notably from the firm of Wente Brothers. In France this grape is called the *Chauche Gris*. It is not related to the German Riesling.

GRIGNOLINO Italian red grape grown in Piedmont and yielding a light pale red wine to be served cool. Also planted in California.

GROS-PLANT Oddly named white grape which produces wine very similar to Muscadet in the same area – the part of the Loire which is near the Brittany coast in France, close to Nantes. Very dry and crisp.

GROSSLAGE German official phrase of a composite vineyard made up of a grouping of various individual vineyards. Examples include Badstube and Kurfurstlay in the Bernkastel area which would give wines called **Bernkasteler Badstube** and **Berkasteler Kurfurstlay**.

H

HALLGARTEN Name of a wine village in the Rheingau area of Germany. Also of a well-known shipper for name/good quality German wines.

HATTENHEIM German wine village in Rheingau region. It includes part of the Marcobrunn estate, one of Germany's finest for excellent **Riesling** white wines, and the Steinberg vineyard.

HAUT-BRION, CHÂTEAU Wine estate in the Graves area of Bordeaux in France. Producing a very fine classified red wine. Expensive.

HAUT-MÉDOC Part of the Médoc area near Bordeaux in France which includes major wine villages such as Margaux and Pauillac. Wines simply labelled **Haut-Médoc** are usually well-made and delicate red wines, better than those simply called **Médoc**. They are a good value when compared with the lesser château-bottled wines which may sell on a fancy label.

HÉRAULT Large wine area in southern France which is most important for table wine, little of which is exported. Also an area for dessert wines such as the **Muscat de Frontignan** and for a few interesting and inexpensive red wines such as **Minervois**.

HERMITAGE A wine beloved of Victorian England and once used to 'beef up' claret, it now is a fine red Rhône wine with a long life span. The most important is the red but white is also a fine very dry wine. Wine made in the surrounding area is called **Crozes-Hermitage**, for the nearby village, and is less expensive.

HESSISCHE BERGSTRASSE Minor German wine region near Baden.

HOCHEIM Origin of the name 'hock', still used in Britain for Rhine wines. This town was a port for shipping wines and is still a centre of production for fine Riesling white wines. One of its most memorable vineyard names is that of **Konigin Victoria** (Queen Victoria).

HOSPICES DE BEAUNE Major Burgundy wine auction held in the small French city of Beaune in November each year. Held partly to aid charity but mostly to fix prices for new wines. The original Hospice de Beaune is a very beautiful mediaeval building in the centre of the city.

HUNGARY The wines from this eastern European country are often well-made and varied. They are shipped to the West by a state monopoly company called Monimpex, which awards a quality seal to each wine. The most famous red wine is probably **Bull's Blood**, known as **Egri Bikavér**, a very heavy sturdy red wine that goes with rich food. The finest white wine is the famous **Tokay** made from the Furmint grape and in fine years a long-lived special golden dessert wine. A good dry white wine is the **Debroi Harslevelu**, and the wines of Badacsony are also considered typical Hungarian white wines. Good value.

HYBRID A grape variety which is a cross between two species, notably the American native *vitis vinifera* and the European *vitis labrusca* yielding such vines as

Brolio castle and vineyards, Chianti district, Italy

the Ruby Cabernet and the Emerald Riesling which adapt well to hot climates and American soils. French hybrids include the Seyval Blanc which does well in England and in the eastern United States.

I

ISRAEL A country with a hot climate best suited to the production of sweeter wines but use of modern techniques is improving the wines all the time. Some European varieties like Cabernet Sauvignon and Semillion are now doing well there. The Carmel Wine Company is the best known for both kosher and regular wines under either brand names or with varietal labels. They also offer a sparkling wine made by the champagne method.

ITALY The 'home of the vine', wine is made everywhere here. Italy is the world's largest wine producer, exporting great amounts to France (much of it for blending), to the US and to Britain as well as to most corners of the globe. Some of the most famous wines are **Chianti,** made in Tuscany, **Soave** and **Valpolicella,** made in the area around Venice and **Bardolino. Lambrusco** is made in Emilia Romagna, **Verdicchio** in the Marche area, **Frascati** near Rome, **Orvieto** from Umbria, and the sweet **Lacryma Christi** from Naples. The most famous fortified wine is **Marsala,** made in Sicily, and **Asti Spumante,** perhaps the most famous sparkling wine, is from Piedmont.

J

JEREZ Town which gives sherry its name. Is still the centre of production in Spain.

JEROBOAM Extra large bottle equal to six standard bottles of Bordeaux wine or four of champagne.

JOHANNISBERG Most famous name in the Rheingau region of Germany, particularly the vineyards of **Schloss Johannisberg**. Produces fine white Riesling wines. In California the Riesling of Germany is called Johannisberg Riesling.

JUG WINE Term used in United States to describe wine (usually generic) sold in large containers at low prices.

JURA Wine region of eastern France near Switzerland where rare white wines, including **Château-Chalon** (a yellow wine rather like dry sherry), are made

from dried grapes, as well as some good rosé and light red wine. Most wine from this region is labelled **Arbois**.

JURANÇON Another rather obscure wine region in southwest France. Best known for rich dry white wines – also some sweeter versions.

K

KABINETT One of the official German wine categories within the top quality designation — *Qualitätswein mit Prädkat (Qmp)*. *Kabinett* means the 'winemaker's own selection', and it is the driest of these

Johannisberg vineyards, Rheingau district, Germany

Left: Sherry poster from Jerez, Spain.

wines and often very good value. A *Kabinett* wine is medium-dry and made with Riesling, Sylvaner, or, occasionally, Müller-Thurgau and other grape varieties.

KASEL German wine village within the Mosel-Saar-Ruwer region. Produces light white wines.

KELLER German word for 'cellar'.

KIEDRICH German wine village in the Rheingau district. Produces some very fine **Riesling** wines both medium-dry and sweet.

KIR Aperitif made with dry white wine and *crème de cassis* liqueur.

KLOSTER EBERBACH Location of annual German wine auction and also of a study centre for learning about the wines of Germany.

KOSHER WINE Wine approved by a Jewish rabbi. Produced in Israel or in other countries, notably the eastern United States, where the Concord grape is commonly used to make a sweet wine.

KREUZNACH Important town in the Nahe region of Germany. Good medium-dry white wines.

101

L

LABRUSCA A type of wine native to the U.S. and still widely grown in the Eastern States. Varieties include the Concord, the Catawba, and the Niagara.

LACRYMA CHRISTI Italian sweet white wine from Naples.

LAFITE-ROTHSCHILD, CHÂTEAU Very famous red wine from Bordeaux in France. Among the top five classified in the Médoc area. This exceptional and complex red wine is very expensive and often bought as an investment.

LAMBRUSCO Popular semi-sparkling red wine made in the province of Emilia Romagna, Italy. The fizz comes from a secondary fermentation in the bottle. Serve cool and drink while still young.

LANGUEDOC Name of a French region where a vast amount of table wine is produced. Areas include the Hérault, Aude, and Gard. Some wine is used for **vermouth** and some for better red wines such as **Fitou** and **Corbières**.

LATOUR, CHÂTEAU A first growth wine like **Lafite**. This is one of the world's most expensive wines and in good years has a subtlety of flavour unequalled in red wines, but at a price which is hard to contemplate. One of the top five Bordeaux reds. The vineyards also yield a second wine called **Les Forts de Latour,** which is less expensive, but distinguished by being aged in bottle three years before it is released.

LAZIO Italian wine region near Rome. Home of **Frascati**.

LIEBFRAUMILCH One of the world's best-selling wines under brand names such as **Blue Nun,** this is a semi-sweet light white wine made in Germany — principally from grapes grown in the Rheinhessen district. It is a pleasant although not very exciting drink. Look for alternatives to the major brands to get better value.

LIMOUX Area in Languedoc in France producing a pleasant medium-dry sparkling wine called **Blanquette de Limoux.**

LIRAC Area of the Rhône Valley best known for quality rosé wines but also good for rich reds.

LOIRE An important French wine region yielding some of the best value wines in France, all of top quality. Names to look for include **Muscadet, Sancerre,** and **Pouilly Fumé** (dry white wines), **Vouvray** (medium-dry), **Anjou rosé** (medium-dry or sweet), **Chinon** and **Bourgeuil** (fruity red wines) and **Coteaux du Layon** (sweet dessert wines). The Loire is also the source of some excellent inexpensive wines such as **Sauvignon de Touraine,** a dry clean white wine, and **Gamay de la Loire,** a very good alternative to **Beaujolais.**

LOMBARDY Italian wine region near Milan, including Lake Garda where various light red wines are made, including **Chiaretto**. Also where the **Frecciarossa** range of wines is produced.

LUGNY Village in France in the Mâcon area, south of the Côte d'Or in Burgundy, which makes good dry white wines called **Mâcon Lugny**.

LUXEMBOURG Minor wine-producing country in Europe. Some good dry sparkling wines.

M

MÂCON Good value wine area, south of the famous Cote d'Or in Burgundy, France. **Mâcon Blanc** is an excellent dry white wine made from the Chardonnay grape, while **Mâcon Rouge** is a smooth agreeable red. **Pouilly Fuissé** is a very popular mid-priced dry white wine.

MADEIRA Volcanic outcrop in the Atlantic Ocean, and home of some unusual fortified wines. Once sent around the world on a sea voyage to get a distinctive 'burnt' flavour but today made by a special process called the *estufa*. Madeira wines are fortified and range from the drier pale styles such as **Sercial** and **Verdelho** to sweet dark rich drinks including **Bual** and **Malmsey**. They were favourites of the early American colonists but today are used for cooking and only occasional drinking. Serve chilled or at room temperture as preferred, after a meal, or as a welcoming drink for guests.

MAGNUM The equivalent of two standard bottles, this holds 1.5 litres.

MALAGA Sweet rich fortified wines made with sun-dried grapes.

MALMSEY The sweetest style of **Madeira**.

MALVASIA White grape widely grown in Italy and made into sweet dessert wines used in **Chianti** in small amounts. In Madeira the grape is called Malmsey. It also does well in Greece, Cryprus, and in California, as well as in the south of France, where it is called *malvoisie*.

MANCHA, LA Very hot area in central Spain where table wine is produced.

MANZANILLA Very light pale dry **sherry** from Spain, made near the sea, which has a distinctive salty flavour.

MARC Pungent grape **brandy** made with the skins of the grapes that remain after they have been pressed for wine. Named after the region of origin such as **Marc de Bourgogne** from Burgundy. Called **grappa** in Italy. Marc is to be found also in the Champagne and Provence wine districts in France.

MARCHE Italian wine region best known for its dry white **Verdicchio**.

MARCOBRUNN Famous German wine estate in the Rheingau district. Perhaps the finest of German white wines are made here under names including **Schloss Rheinhartshausen** and **Schloss Schönborn**.

MARGAUX Village in Haut-Médoc near Bordeaux, France producing some of the finest and most elegant wines from this celebrated region. Among Margaux's famous red wines are **Château Lascombes**, **Château Palmer**, **Château Brane-Cantenac**, and **Château Prieuré-Lichine**. Do not confuse the *AC* commune **Margaux** with the legendary **Château Margaux**, a first-growth wine of exceptional quality. As one of the top five Bordeaux reds, it is very expensive.

MARSALA Italian fortified wine made in Sicily. Sold in various grades – *superiore* is usually available and this may be flavoured with eggs. Use for cooking or an after dinner drink.

MAXIMIN GRÜNHAUS Very celebrated wine estate in the Mosel-Saar-Ruwer.

MÉDOC The most expensive and famous area of Bordeaux for red wines. Home of four of the five top châteaux: **Ch. Latour, Ch. Lafite, Ch. Mouton-Rothschild,** and **Ch. Margaux**, as well as all the other classified growths. Wine simply labelled **Médoc** is usually from the Bas Médoc in the north of the region and then there is **Haut Médoc**, the area surrounding the famous villages of St.-Estèphe, Pauillac, Margaux and St.-Julien. The major grape varieties grown here are the Cabernet Sauvignon, Cabernet Franc, Merlot and Malbec, with some Petit Verdot. Other important villages are Ludon, Listrac and Moulis. Any wine may be labelled with a village name if it is produced in the area but is not necessarily a château-bottled wine. The 'commune' wines can be very good value.

MENDOCINO California wine country north of Napa and Sonoma with quite a cool climate. Wineries include Fetzer and Parducci.

MERCUREY A fine French wine made in the southern part of Burgundy from Pinot Noir. Good value.

MERLOT Fruity rich red grape grown in all parts of the wine world but most famous in St. Emilion and Pomerol in Bordeaux, France. Also makes good wine in northern Italy, in Switzerland and in California. Merlot is at its best when blended with Cabernet Sauvignon.

MÉTHODE CHAMPENOISE The gradual process of putting bubbles in champagne by fermenting the wine in its bottle. As some stages are done by hand and involve much time and money the price of fine champagne is inevitably high. The method is also now used in the production of some sparkling wines in France and elsewhere which are outside the Champagne district.

METHUSELAH Extra large bottle size for champagne – equals eight bottles.

MEURSAULT Famous district in France for producing white Burgundy with a very rich buttery aroma. Vineyards located here include **Perrières** and **Charmes**. The vineyard name is added to the village name. Expensive.

MEXICO A hot climate country but some good wines are made here as well as a good deal of brandy. Wineries include Santo Tomas and San Lorenzo as well as Domecq, the sherry company.

MICHIGAN More important for table grapes than wine but some wines are made with hybrid varieties near the town of Paw Paw.

MINERVOIS Good country red wine from the south of France. Very good value VDQS quality.

MEDOC

APPELLATION MEDOC CONTROLEE

GRAND VIN DE BORDEAUX

75 cl

M Brette

négociant à Bordeaux Gironde FRANCE

Champagne sediment after second fermentation in the bottle which must be carefully removed before rebottling and corking

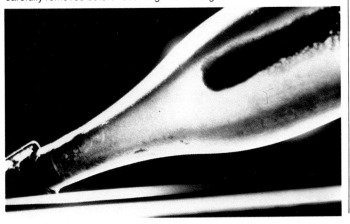

MISSOURI Native varieties predominate in these American vineyards, but experiments with hybrids are now under way.

MONBAZILLAC Sweet white dessert wine made near Bergerac in France. Good alternative to **Sauternes**.

MONTAGNY White wine made in France in southern Burgundy. Similar to **Mâcon Blanc** (made with the Chardonnay grape); moderately priced.

MONTEPULCIANO Home of the **Vino Nobile**, a red wine which is prized by connoisseurs, in the Tuscany region of Italy.

MONTEREY California wine county outstanding for white wines such as **Riesling**. Centre for experimentation. Paul Masson is an important producer as is Monterey Vineyard. The **Chardonnay** wines of **Chalone** are highly regarded.

MONTILLA A rival to sherry in Spain and very good value – comes in the same grades of sweetness. Montilla wines are not usually fortified, however.

MONTRACHET Famous white Burgundy considered the best by most experts. The most important vineyard is, simply, Montrachet. Chevalier-Montrachet, Bâtard-Montrachet, and other top vineyards are also in the surrounding area. The local village name is **Puligny-Montrachet** and these wines can be good value white burgundies in a plentiful year. Neighbouring **Chassagne-**

Vineyards in Château Lefagé, Monbazillac, France

Montrachet is best known for red wines. The white wines are made with Chardonnay and the red with Pinot Noir.

MOREY ST DENIS Fine red Burgundy village with vineyards including **Clos St. Denis, Clos de la Roche**, and part of **Bonnes-Mares**. All produce very elegant and expensive red Burgundies.

MORGON One of the nine named French villages in the Beaujolais district. Makes quite a rich wine.

MOSCATEL, MOSCATO Wines made with muscat grapes which are sweet and may be fortified. **Moscatel de Setubal** from Portugal is fortified, while **Muscato Mabile** from California is a dessert wine.

MOSEL One of the two foremost German wine regions. The other is the Rheingau. Mosel wines are loved by experts for their fresh yet fragrant style, made from the Riesling grape. The climate is cool and the wines are light and acidic yet have some sweetness. Famous names include **Bernkastel, Piesport, Graach, Wehlen, Zeltingen**, and individual vineyard such as **Maximin Grünhaus**. For official purposes the full name of the region is the Mosel-Saar-Ruwer, all names of rivers.

MOSELBLÜMCHEN Equivalent to **Liebfraumilch**. Produced in the Mosel rather than the Rhine area. It is only a *tafelwein* (table wine) and can be sickly sweet.

MOSELLE French word for German Mosel.

MOULIN-À-VENT One of the nine named Beaujolais villages

in France.

MOULIS Village in the Médoc, Bordeaux, with some very fine second-rank red wines (not 'classed growths') such as **Château Chasse-Spleen**.

MOUSSEUX Fizzy. The term *vin mousseux* means sparkling wine and is used for all French sparkling wines which are made outside the official Champagne area, e.g. **sparkling Vouvray**.

MOUTON-ROTHSCHILD, CHÂTEAU The only Bordeaux wine to be re-classified since the list of Médoc châteaux was drawn up in 1855. Now a 'first growth'. Mouton-Rothschild is rare and expensive red claret. The estate also produces **Château Mouton-Baronne-Philippe** (named for the late wife of the owner), a good value fine Bordeaux, and the international brand **Mouton Cadet** which is available in red and white styles. Both are dry.

MÜLLER-THURGAU A grape type which is the result of a cross between the Riesling and Sylvaner varieties. Does well in southern Germany and in Great Britain for soft, light white wines.

MUSCADET Very popular dry white wine called 'the poor man's Chablis' as it goes well with seafood and is bone dry like its aristocratic cousin. Muscadet *sur lie* is a wine which has been allowed to rest on the lees, or sediment of spent yeast cells, after fermentation and gain extra flavour. Good value wine from the Loire region of France. Muscadet is also the name of a type of grape.

MUSCAT Distinctive spicy table grape used for sweet wines.

Muscat grape

MUSCATEL Wines made with the Muscat grape, sometimes fortified. In the US, many of such fortified wines are not of very high quality.

MUSIGNY In Burgundy in France, this is an important vineyard for very delicate red wines. The nearby village name is **Chambolle-Musigny**, and this wine is less expensive but still a very fine red wine from the Pinot Noir grape, said to smell of violets.

MUST Technical word for grape juice.

N

NAHE German wine region named from a tributary of the Rhine river. Best-known names here are **Schloss Böckelheim** and **Kreuznach**, and the wines are all typical white Rhine wines made with Riesling and Sylvaner.

NAPA Most famous valley in the California wine country with

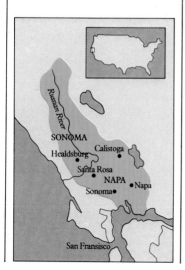

many excellent wineries including Beaulieu, Beringer, Charles Krug, Robert Mondavi, Louis Martini, Sterling Vineyards, Chappellet, Freemark Abbey, Stag's Leap, and Clos du Val. The climate here is ideal for grape growing as it is warm in the day and cooler at night, with sheltered hillsides. Grape types which do well include the Chardonnay and Johannisberg Riesling for white wines, but all styles are made here, including fine 'champagne' at Schramsberg and Hanns Kornell.

NEBBIOLO Important red wine grape of Piedmont in Italy used to made **Barolo** and **Barbaresco**.

Mechanical grape harvester used at Trefethen vineyards, Napa Valley, California

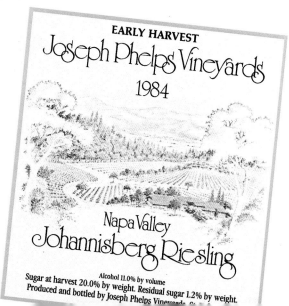

EARLY HARVEST
Joseph Phelps Vineyards
1984

Napa Valley
Johannisberg Riesling

Alcohol 11.0% by volume
Sugar at harvest 20.0% by weight. Residual sugar 1.2% by weight.
Produced and bottled by Joseph Phelps Vineyards, C...

NEW YORK STATE After California, the second most important region of production in the United States. Sparkling wines are a major part of the production by companies such as Gold Seal and Taylors. Table wines can suffer from extreme weather conditions but hybrid and native varieties do well, including the famous Concord and Delaware, Niagara, etc. (native vines) and Chelois, Seyval Blanc and Foch (hybrids). Some New York wines are blended with California wines to add smoothness. The Finger Lakes are a centre of production where, apart from those mentioned, other wineries include Pleasant Valley, which makes the popular **Great Western** sparkling wine, Vinifera Wine Cellars, which use only European varieties, Bully Hill, Canandaigua Industries, which has brands including **Virginia Dare** and **Wild Irish Rose** and Boordy Vineyards, specialising in wines made with hybrid vines. Other areas in New York State include the Chautauqua area near Lake Erie and the Hudson River Valley where the Brotherhood winery is based.

NEW ZEALAND The two islands of New Zealand lie on the same latitude in the southern hemisphere as Bordeaux and Burgundy in France so the prospects for fine wine making are good. Exports are rising at present for wines made with the **Chardonnay**, **Riesling** and **Gewürztraminer** (white wines); and the **Cabernet Sauvignon** and **Pinot Noir** (red wines). Producers to watch for include **Cook's**, **Glenvale**, **Montana**, **McWilliams** and **Penfolds**. As a general rule, the wines of New Zealand are

NIERSTEIN Very well-known wine village in the Rheinhessen district of Germany with fruity white wines which appeal to all tastes. They include simple **Niersteiner** as well as **Niersteiner Gütes Domtal**, made from Riesling and Sylvaner grapes.

NOSE Taster's word for the smell of a wine.

NUITS-ST-GEORGES Town name and one of the French Burgundies most familiar to wine lovers. Gives its name to the Côte de Nuits, that part of Burgundy most renowned for red wines from the Pinot Noir grape.

O

OCKFEN Important wine village in the Mosel-Saar-Ruwer area of Germany which makes one special wine called **Ockfener Bockstein** and other lesser wines. All are white and very rich in taste.

somewhat lighter than those of Australia and less alcoholic. The principal production zones are Hawkes' Bay and Auckland in the North Island, and Blenheim in the South Island.

COOKS

COOKS NEW ZEALAND WINE COMPANY LIMITED.

OHIO American wine region with some vineyards along the Ohio river and others on the shores of Lake Erie. The largest producer is Meiers Wine Cellars in Cincinatti. Most wines are made with native American grape varieties though some hybrids have now been planted.

OLOROSO Rich dark **sherry** from Spain which may occasionally be dry but is usually quite sweet. **Cream sherry** is made with full oloroso. A fortified wine.

OPPENHEIM Major Rheinhessen wine town in Germany.

OREGON A new and exciting wine region for America with some fine delicate wines being made from traditional European varieties. White **Riesling, Cabernet Sauvignon** and **Pinot Noir** are among the promising varieties being developed.

ORVIETO Well-known white wine made in the Umbria region of Italy. Made from various white grape varieties including Trebbiano and Malvasia. It was formerly sold in flasks like **Chianti** but costs have risen and now bottles are more usual. The dry version is labelled *secco* and the sweeter is *abbocato*.

P

PAARL Major wine region of South Africa. Best known winery is the KWV Wine Association, making wines, sherries and brandy.

PASSE-TOUT-GRAINS Red wine of Burgundy made with a blend of Pinot Noir and Gamay grapes. Light and relatively inexpensive.

PAUILLAC One of the major wine villages of the Bordeaux Médoc. Home of **Château Latour** and **Château Lafite** and **Mouton-Rothschild** as well as **Château Pontet-Canet, Château Picon-Longueville Lalande,** and **Château Batailley.**

PÉTILLANT French for a slightly sparkling wine.

PETIT CHABLIS Wine made in the Chablis area of France but not of the first rank. Less expensive and less exciting than the real thing but worth trying.

PETIT VERDOT Minor red grape variety used in Bordeaux red wine.

PETITE SIRAH American name of a grape originally from the Rhône in France but not the same as the Syrah. Makes full rich red wine.

PÉTRUS, CHÂTEAU One of the world's most expensive and rare red wines. Made in the Pomerol area of Bordeaux in France and prized by investors as well as drinkers. Very rich with a long life. Mainly made with Merlot.

PHYLLOXERA Vine louse which destroyed virtually all European vineyards in the 19th century until it was discovered that native American species are resistant to the insect's ravages. The solution was to graft European vines onto American rootstock, a practice which is still followed today as a safeguard against future *phylloxera* attacks. Pre-*phylloxera* wine is rare and expensive and wine buffs boast of its superiority over wine from grafted vines.

PIEDMONT English way of saying *Piemonte*. Northern Italian region where **Barolo, Barbaresco, Asti Spumante,** and other good wines are made.

PIESPORT Wine village in the Mosel region of Germany which is source of various popular wines. Includes **Piesporter Michelsberg** and **Piesporter Goldtropfchen**. These white wines are fragrant and may be medium-dry or sweet depending on their grading.

PINOT Group of grape varieties including the Pinot Noir of Burgundy in France and the Pinot Blanc grown in Alsace and Germany, as well as minor Pinot Meunier. Pinot

Right: Vineyards in the Piedmont region of Italy

Pinot Blanc grape

Chardonnay is a misnomer – it should be simply Chardonnay.

PINOT GRIGIO Grape variety popular in north-eastern Italy which makes fairly full-flavoured white wines carrying the same name. **Collio Goriziano** is one of the best examples.

POMEROL Wine village in the Bordeaux region of France which makes very expensive and special red wine including **Château Pétrus, Château La Fleur-Pétrus,** and **Château Gazin,** among others. There is not an official classification of Pomerol wines, but they are made in small amounts and are invariably expensive but worth the investment.

POMMARD Famous name in Burgundy, France for very full red wine with a long life. Easy to say in English, always popular and unfortunately overpriced.

PORT A fortified wine which technically comes from the area around Oporto in northern Portugal but is much imitated in countries including the United States, South Africa, and Australia. The various standard styles include a dry **white** port, a rich **ruby** port, a smoother **tawny** port, and more expensive wines such as **aged tawny** and **vintage** port, which are expensive and need at least ten years of ageing before drinking. Good buys are **Late Bottled Vintage** (LBV) which has a full style but is not as rare and heavy as vintage —

and lower priced. Notable port shippers include Taylors, Dow, Warre, Fonseca and Croft.

POUILLY-FUISSÉ Popular French white wine made in the southern part of the Burgundy region from the Chardonnay grape. Unfortunately, now in such demand that prices have risen.

POUILLY-FUMÉ Not to be confused with the wine above, this is made many miles away in the Loire Valley and is very dry and crisp with a typical 'gunflint' Sauvignon Blanc aroma. Perfect with seafood.

POUILLY-SUR-LOIRE Lesser wine from the same village as **Pouilly Fumé** but made with a fruitier grape type.

POUILLY-LOCHÉ, POUILLY-VINZELLES, Cousins of **Pouilly Fuissé,** good value.

PROVENCE Region of southern France where pleasant red and rosé wines of medium quality are made. Best are **Bandol,** full and red, and **Cassis,** a light white wine. Not much is

• •

PORTUGAL Many wine drinkers may know of Portuguese wine because of **Mateus** or **Lancers rosé** but there is far more to try than just those light fruity wines. The very dry **Vinho Verde** is unusual and

very refreshing, and the rich red and white wines of the **Dão** region are good value for those who like a heavy wine. There is **port** and **Madeira** for the traditionalist.

exported.

PULIGNY-MONTRACHET
Wine village in the Côte de Beaune area of Burgundy in France where the great **Montrachet** wine is made and its various relatives including **Chevalier-Montrachet** and others. Wine simply called **Puligny-Montrachet** will be the least expensive but still not cheap. Very fine and subtle Chardonnay.

Q

QUALITÄTSWEIN Under German wine law, the better wines are either *Qualitätswein bestimmter Anbaugebiete* (*QbA*) or *Qualitätswein mit Prädikat* (*QmP*). The word means 'quality wine' i.e. better than table wine (*tafelwein*).

QUARTS DE CHAUME
Unusual sweet wine made in small amounts in the Loire region of France from Chenin Blanc grapes.

QUINTA Portuguese term meaning 'estate'. Each port shipper has several of these, yielding wines which are aged and bottled after blending in Oporto.

R

RAINWATER A drier style of **Madeira**.

RAUENTHAL Important Rheingau wine village making full spicy white wines from the Riesling grape.

RECIOTO Wine made in the Veneto region of Italy. Grapes are dried, then added to the basic wine for greater sweetness. The usual names found abroad are **Valpolicella** and **Soave** in this style.

RESERVA Spanish word for 'reserve'. A superior wine – usually red which has been aged for longer than usual in the cask.

RETSINA Greek wine (the majority of their production) which has resin added. The wine may be rosé or white.

RHEINGAU Centre of the Rhine wine production in Germany and home of the finest names, such as **Schloss Johannisberg**. Important towns and villages here include Rauenthal, Eltville, Erbach, Kiedrich, Hattenheim, Hallgarten, Winkel, Geisenheim, and Rüdesheim. Major estates for fine and rare Riesling wines

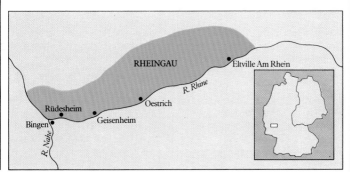

include **Schloss Vollrads** and **Steinberg**.

RHEINHESSEN Region producing lesser-quality wines than the Rheingau but more accessible in price. Many made with the fast-ripening 'soft' flavoured Müller-Thurgau grape. Apart from **Liebfraumilch**, names to watch for include **Nierstein, Nackenheim, Oppenheim, Deinheim**, and **Bodenheim**.

RHEINPFALZ Also known as the Palatinate, this is a vast German production region for the mid-quality wines. Major names are **Durkheim, Forst, Deidesheim, Wachenheim**, and **Ruppertsberg**. Quality varies and the style is slightly more subtle than in the Rheinhessen.

RHÔNE The Rhône flows through both France and Italy, but it is in the area south of Lyons, toward Marseille, that

Vineyards in the Rheinhessen region, Germany

notable wines are made. The most widely sold is simply called **Côtes du Rhône** which may be red, white or rosé, but as a rule appears as red. Full and with a pleasant 'earthy' taste, this wine may be made from grapes grown anywhere in the region. Often good value. Finer red wines include **Côte Rotie**, **Hermitage** and **Crozes-Hermitage**, **Châteauneuf-du-Pape**, **Gigondas**, and **Lirac**. All have richness which needs some years of ageing to appreciate. Allow them to 'breathe' by decanting before serving. The dry white wines are also rich and full. They include **Condrieu**, the rare **Château Grillet**, and white **Hermitage**. The best rosé is orangey in colour and comes from **Tavel**

and **Lirac**. Sparkling wines are made at **Saint-Péray** and Die – the latter called **Clairette de Die**. The dessert wine called **Muscat de Beaumes de Venise** is very good – it tastes of apricots.

RIESLING A famous grape variety used to make the fine white wines of Germany. Also very successful in Austria, Alsace in France, in Australia, California, and South Africa. Some wines are fruity yet dry (Alsace), and others are medium-dry (Rhine and Mosel wines). A few are rich and sweet because they are affected by the so-called noble rot (*Auslese* and *Beerenauslese* wines of Germany and some late-harvest California wines). Other grapes also called Riesling are not the true Johannisberg Riesling. The Emerald Riesling, for instance, is a hybrid developed in California. Riesling wines are also widely made in Eastern Europe. Yugoslavia produces an excellent and inexpensive medium-dry white wine at **Lutomer**.

RIOJA Vast wine-producing region along the River Ebro in the north of Spain whose wines gain in popularity each year. The red wines have some of the complex quality of French claret, with a vanilla scent which comes from ageing in American oak casks. Important shippers include **Bodegas Bilbainas**, **Marqués de Riscal**, **Marqués de Murrietta**, and **CUNE**. White wines are also sold. They may be light and dry or made the traditional way by ageing in oak like red wines to give a pungent flavour. The top wines are aged for several years and called *reserva*. The wines are made

from blends of various grape types – notably Grenache for the red wines and Malvasia for the whites. Wines with the label **Rioja Alta** are usually among the finest of the red and white wines from this region.

RISERVA Italian word for 'reserve' – a superior wine which has been aged over several years.

ROMANÉE-CONTI Famous French vineyard in Burgundy, making rare, very rich red wine which sells for extraordinary prices. Apart from **Romanée-Conti**, and other wines made in La Romanée vineyards are **La Tâche**, **Echézeaux**, **Richebourg**, **Grands-Echézeaux**, and **Romanée-St.-Vivant**. A major shipper of these wines and all fine burgundies is Louis Latour.

ROMANIA Wines made in this socialist country are marketed by an agency called Vinexport. They include varietals such as **Muscat, Riesling, Pinot Noir,** and **Cabernet** as well as a famous dessert wine called **Cotnari**. Quality is quite high, though perhaps not as good as nearby Bulgaria.

Riesling grape

ROSADO Spanish word for rosé.

ROSATO Italian word for rosé.

ROSÉ Wine made by leaving the skins of red grapes in brief contact with the fermenting juice. Best world rosés are from Anjou and the southern Rhone in France (e.g., **Lirac**); from California, and an enormous quantity is made in Portugal under brand names such as **Mateus Rosé**.

ROSSO Italian word for 'red'. In **vermouth** it means a sweet style.

ROUSSILLON The red wines called **Côtes de Roussillon** are good value. They are made in southern France near Spain.

RUBY CABERNET Hybrid grape variety developed in California by crossing the Carignane and the Cabernet Sauvignon. Not to be confusd with the noble Cabernet Sauvignon. Makes a strong dry red wine.

RÜDESHEIM German wine town in the Reingau district. Many vineyards are planted on steep slopes and called 'berg' such as Berg Rottland and Berg Roseneck. The white wines made here are rich and fruity.

RULLY French red and white wines made in southern Burgundy from Chardonnay and Pinot Noir. The dry white wines are good alternatives to white burgundy, and there are also well-made sparkling wines.

RUPPERTSBERG Noted wine town in the Rheinpfalz. Soft delicate white wines. Important vineyards are Gaisböhl and Hoheburg.

RUWER Part of the Mosel-Saar-Ruwer district in Germany, including the **Maximin Grünhaus** wine estate. Good wine is also made at Kasel and Abelsback. All very light and delicate.

S

SAAR Part of the Mosel-Saar-Ruwer district in Germany named from the river of the same name. Notable wines (all white and made with Riesling grape) include **Scharzhofberg, Ockfener Bockstein, Ayler Kupp**, and the wines of **Wiltingen**.

SAINT-EMILION Attractive wine town in the Bordeaux region of France renowned for its full red wines, notably **Château Cheval Blanc**, and **Château Ausone**, the two *premier grand crus* of the 1954 Official Classification. This category also includes a secondary section of top wines such as **Château Beauséjour, Château Canon, Château Figeac, Château Magdelaine, Château Pavie**, and **Château La Gaffelière**. After this come the *grand crus classés* including good wine such as **Clos des Jacobins** and **Château La Tour Figeac**. Finally there are dozens of so-called *grand crus* some of which are not particularly good. At its best St. Emilion is rich and full with all the fruit and acidity of the Merlot grape.

SAINT-ESTEPHE Wine village in the Médoc area of Bordeaux, France. Fine red wines made here include many *crus classés* such as **Château Cos d'Estournel, Château Calon-Ségur**, and **Château Lafon-Rochet**. Some other châteaux,

Saint -Emilion vineyards near Bordeaux, France

which are not classified, are often very good value such as **Château Meyney** (which belongs to Cordier) and **Château Phelan-Ségur**. The wine style here is said to be earthier than that of the other Médoc villages.

SAINT-JULIEN Another of the top Médoc wine villages. Home to **Château Léoville-Las-Cases, Château Léoville-Poyferré, Château Léoville-Barton,** and **Château Ducru-Beaucaillou** among others. A notable 'non-classified' wine is **Château Gloria,** considered worthy of classification. The wines made here are full and dry reds.

SAINT-VÉRAN. Fairly new *appellation* in the Mâcon district of southern Burgundy for good dry white wines from the Chardonnay grape.

SANCERRE Famous name which unfortunately now costs more than it should. A very dry crisp wine made in the Loire Valley in France from Sauvignon

Saumur sparkling wine

Blanc grapes. Try Pouilly-Fumé as an alternative.

SANGIOVESE Italian red grape type used in making **Chianti** and **Brunello di Montalcino**, among others.

SANGRIA Wine punch made with red wine and oranges, originating in Spain. Sometimes sold ready-mixed.

SANTA CLARA California county which is home to wineries including **Paul Masson, Mirassou, San Martin,** and **Almaden**, as well as family-owned wineries like **Guglielmo. Ridge Vineyard** is famous for Zinfandel wines and **David Bruce** is a winemaking doctor.

SANTENAY French wine village at the southern limit of the Côte d'Or in Burgundy for smooth red wines which can be good value.

SARDINIA Italian island which makes undistinguished wines, but its **Vernaccia di Oristano** is a pleasant dry white wine.

SAUMUR Loire wine town in France which makes good dry white wines as well as some fruity red **(Saumur-Champigny)** and excellent sparkling wine by the champagne method.

SAUTERNES A much-borrowed name for sweet white wine which should only apply to particular French wine made south of Bordeaux from grapes affected by *botrytis* (the noble rot). Names to look for include the legendary **Château d'Yquem, Château Rieussec, Château Doisy-Daëne,** and **Château de Suduiraut.** The neighbouring village of Barsac makes fine wines including **Château Coutet** and **Château Climens.** In America, the name Sauternes may be applied misleadingly to all styles of white wine.

SAUVIGNON BLANC White grape type is used in making French **Sauternes, Sancerre,** and other sweet and dry wines. Does well in California where it is often labelled **Fumé Blanc**. French wines called **Sauvignon** are often dry light white wines and good value (such as **Sauvignon de Touraine**).

SAVENNIÈRES Loire wine village which makes delicate yet rich dry white wines, notably **La Roche aux Moines**.

SCHARZHOFBERG Saar vineyard which is famous for complex white **Riesling** wines. Expensive.

SCHLOSS German for 'castle'. e.g., Schloss Johannisberg, Schloss Bockelheim.

SCUPPERNONG Native American grape type which thrives in the southern states.

SEC French for 'dry'.

SECO Spanish for 'dry'.

SECCO Italian for 'dry'.

SEDIMENT The deposit found at the bottom of some bottles of wine. particularly well-aged or full-bodied red wines, One of the purposes of decanting some bottles of red wine or port is to remove the sediment.

SEIBEL Hybrid grape variety grown in the United States.

SEKT German sparkling wine make with the Riesling grape. Good and fruity, mid-priced. Brands include **Henkell trocken**.

SEMILLON White grape used in making of Sauternes in France. Also does well in Australia and California.

SERCIAL Dry style of **Madeira**. Fortified wine.

SEYBE-VILLARD Hybrid grape

Semillon grape

type grown in the United States, in France, and in England.

SHERRY Fortified wine made principally in the town of Jerez, Spain, in various styles including *fino* (dry), *amontillado* (medium), and *oloroso* and cream (sweet). Other countries making good 'sherry' include Australia, Cyprus, South Africa and the United States. Leading Spanish shippers include Domecq, Gonzalez Byass, and Williams and Humbert. A good deal of Spanish sherry is sold under brand names such as **Tio Pepe, Dry Sack**.

SICILY Noted for fortified **Marsala**, this Italian island also produces **Etna** and **Corvo** table wines.

SOAVE Light Italian white wine which is very popular. Good value drinking.

SONOMA California wine country near Napa and north to San Francisco. Wineries here include **Chateau St. Jean, Sebastiani, Simi**, and **Pedroncelli** as well as **Buena Vista**, one of the the state's oldest wineries.

SOUTH AFRICA This country has an ideal wine growing climate and exports excellent wines at good prices. Look for the brands **KWV** and **Nederburg** as well as **Fleur du Cap** for value. Varietals include **Cabernet Sauvignon, Shiraz** and **Cinsaut** (red), and **Riesling, Colombard, Clairette** and **Steen** (white). Style is usually rich and full like the wines of California, but they also make true dessert wines which are labelled 'late harvest' and good 'sherries'. Each year a major wine auction is held at the **Nederburg** Estate which realises high prices for fine and rare South African wines. Nederburg is in the Stellenbosch area; the other major areas are Constantia. (where a famous sweet wine is still made); Tulbagh; Paarl; the little Karoo; and to the north the less important Olifants River area.

• •

SOVIET UNION A major world wine producer, but most is consumed at home. *Shampanskoe* or sparkling wine is very popular and most wines are rather sweet. Georgia is a major production area.

• •

SPAIN Perhaps best known for its range of **sherries** (fortified wines), but Spain also makes excellent table wines such as the smooth red and white **Rioja** and the full wines from Penedès, as well as traditional dessert wines like **Malaga**. One of the rarest and finest red wines is **Vega Sicilia**. Other regions include La Mancha which produces chiefly house wine, and Valdepenas, which makes good drinking wine, red and white. Until recently, the fashion was to make all Spanish wine (even white wines) in a heavy style, aged in wood barrels. But today modern taste has meant a new lighter flavour and the **white Rioja**, for instance, is very crisp and agreeable, as are the white wines of **Torres**, made in Penedès near Barcelona. Names to look for apart from Torres include **Berberana, Domecq** (also famous for sherry), **Campo Viejo, Marqués de Cáceres, Marqués de Riscal** and **Paternina** for **Rioja**; **Codorniu** and **Freixenet** for excellent sparkling wines made by the champagne method.

Right: Vineyards in the Rioja district of Spain

Left: Measuring the degree of alcohol in wine at a Spanish bodega

French table wine

SPANNA Italian red wine from Piedmont made with Nebbiolo. A heavy style.

SPÄTLESE A German wine category for quality wine (*QmP*), meaning the wine is made with especially ripe grapes. These white wines are medium-dry or semi-sweet according to vintage.

SPUMANTE Italian for 'sparkling', as in **Asti Spumante**.

STAATSWEINGUT Means 'state wine domain' in German. Examples include the Steinberg and those in Eltville and Trier. The wines are very good examples of their particular district.

STEEN A grape from South Africa, very similar to Chenin Blanc, which is used to make most of the best of South Africa's dry white wines.

SWITZERLAND The majority of Swiss wine is consumed at home, but some is exported, including the delicate white **Fendant** and the red **Dôle**. Unfortunately, due to currency rates, they are generally expensive.

SYLVANER White grape type mainly grown in Germany where its softness is a contrast to the Riesling. Also grown in Alsace and in California.

SYRAH The great red wine grape of the Rhône Valley which is used in **Châteauneuf-du-Pape, Hermitage,** and other full red wines. It has an aroma of black pepper.

T

TABLE WINE This is generally used to refer to a wine of less than 15° suitable for serving with meals, i.e. not a fortified wine. In Europe's Economic Community the term has a particular legal meaning.

TÂCHE, LA One of the fine French vineyards in the Romanée area of Burgundy. A tiny and expensive corner of this district making exceptional red wines.

TAFELWEIN German for 'table wine'. The simplest style made, rarely exported.

TANNIN The astringent quality of a wine (usually red) which comes from the skins of the grapes and from the wood casks.

TASTEVIN Small metal cup used by tasters in Burgundy, France.

TAVEL Fine orange-tinted rosé

wine made in the Rhône region of France.

THOMPSON SEEDLESS Blending grape variety also sold as table grapes in California.

TINTO Spanish for 'red'. *Vino tinto* is a red wine.

TOKAY Historic sweet white wine of Hungary made with the Furmint grape among others – affected by the 'noble rot' – as in true Sauternes. The top vintages are sold as **Aszu**, referring to these special grapes. The rarest wine is called **Essencia** but this is rarely sold today – the name has been borrowed in California for **Zinfandel Essense**, a late-harvest wine. The wine called Tokay in Alsace is not related and is quite dry. The general style of Tokay is copied in California in a fortified wine.

TOURAINE Province in the Loire Valley, France, the name of which is used for certain wines, such as, **Sauvignon de Touraine**, a light dry white wine.

TREBBIANO Italian white grape used for **Soave** and **Orvieto**, among others. In France it is called the Ugni Blanc.

TRENTINO Italian wine region in the north, associated with the Alto Adige, making good smooth red wines from the Cabernet and Merlot grape types.

TRIER German wine town in the Mosel region where many wine shippers are based.

TROCKENBEERENAUSLESE The finest and rarest of German wines. Very sweet and made with individually picked Riesling grapes affected by the *Edelfäule*, the 'noble rot'.

TUSCANY Italian wine region centred on Siena and Florence making **Chianti, Brunello di Montalcino, Vino Nobile de Montepulciano** (red wines), and a sweet dessert wine called **Vin Santo** from semi-dried grapes, among others.

U

UGNI BLANC Grape type grown in southern France and in the Cognac region. Makes light white wines and is used for blends.

UMBRIA Italian wine area best known for **Orvieto**, a white wine medium-dry or semi-sweet.

ÜRZIG German wine town on the Mosel. Best wine is **Ürziger Würzgarten**.

V

VACQUEYRAS A French wine-producing village in the Côtes du Rhône producing pleasant, less heavy wines than that of its neighbour, **Châteauneuf-du-Pape**.

VALAIS Swiss wine region for red and white wines such as the **Dôle** (red) and **Fendant** (white).

VALDEPENAS Spanish wine region in the La Mancha area where light red and white wines are made, some exported. There is also a grape with this name grown in California.

Harvesting grapes in the Piedmont district, Italy

VALPOLICELLA Popular light Italian red wine made near Lake Garda. Serve cool and when young – under five years old. A slightly sweeter version is called **Recioto,** and a full dry version is **Amarone.**

VALTELLINA Italian wine region making red wines from the Nebbiolo grape as in Piedmont. Wines include **Inferno** and **Sassella,** and **Valgella.**

VARIETAL Word used first in the United States and now elsewhere on wine labels to describe a wine according to grape type, e.g., **Cabernet Sauvignon,** rather than by

château or brand name.

VDQS Means *Vin Délimité de Qualité Supérieure.* – French legal term for next-best to *appellation controlée.* Good local wines such as **Corbiéres** are so designated.

VEGA SICILIA Rare red Spanish wine which has a long life span.

VENDANGE Means 'harvest' in French; the Spanish term is *vendemia,* and in Italian it is *vendemmia.* On a wine label, it indicates the vintage date.

VENEGAZZÙ Italian red and

white wines made in the Veneto region. Good value Bordeaux-style red and white made with Riesling and Pinot.

VENETO Italian wine region to the west of Venice which produces **Bardolino** and **Vapolicella** (red wines) as well as the popular white **Soave**.

VENTOUX, CÔTES DE Good value full-flavoured wines made near the Rhône in France – red, white and rosé.

VERDELHO Medium-dry Madeira. A fortified wine.

VERDICCHIO Light dry white wine from the Marches district of Italy.

VERMOUTH Fortified wine made in a variety of styles with added herbs for flavour. Sweet is called *rosso* in Italy, and the dry is commonly known as 'French', although these wines are now made worldwide. Other styles include *bianco* (medium-sweet white) and rosé. Top Italian producers are **Martini** and **Cinzano**, and in France, **Noilly Prat**.

VERNACCIA Name of an Italian white grape used for wine both sweet and dry including the pleasant **Vernaccia di San Gimignano** made in Tuscany.

VIEILLES VIGNES A French term meaning 'old vines'. These are the ones producing the best wines. When the term is seen on the label of a bottle as it is with certain French wines, for example, from Champagne, Burgundy and Alsace, it should be regarded as an indication of quality.

VIN French word for 'wine'.

VIN DE PAYS A legal definition in France for a good country wine which is not the top rank. Increasingly exported and very good value for money.

VIN SANTO Sweet Italian white wine made with semi-dried grapes.

VINHO VERDE Portuguese light dry white wine with a slight sparkle. The grape are harvested when still unripe, hence *verde,* 'green'.

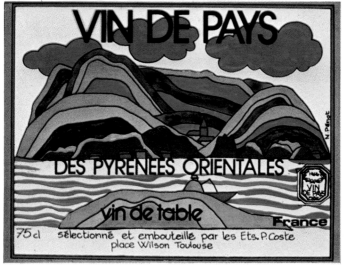

131

VINIFERA The European vine, as opposed to native American varieties.

VINO Word for 'wine' in Italian or Spanish.

VINO NOBILE DI MONTEPULCIANO Fine red wine of Tuscany, Italy.

VINTAGE The date of the harvest. Seen on wines which are of good quality. Naturally, weather conditions mean that vintages can vary according to region and even vineyard. In the port area, only the finest years are 'declared' as a vintage. This is also true of champagne.

VIRE One of the best white wine villages in Mâcon, France.

VOLLRADS, SCHLOSS Famous German wine estate in the Rheingau district.

VOLNAY Notable red Burgundy made near Pommard and Meursault. Considered especially light and subtle – a 'feminine' wine.

VOSNE-ROMANÉE Burgundy wine village in France where all the fine wines of the Romanée vineyard, such as **La Tâche**, are made, as well as wines labelled with the village name. Expensive as a rule.

VOUGEOT Burgundy wine village in France famed for its vineyard, **Clos de Vougeot**. An expensive red wine considered among the top Burgundies.

VOUVRAY Fruity white wine from the Loire, France. Sometimes semi-sweet

• •

VINTAGE CHART

This is not the answer to every query you may have about the vintage of a wine, but should help when selecting a good bottle to serve at home.

KEY: VG: excellent   G: good   F: fair   P: poor, year

REGION	YEARS									
	1975	1976	1977	1978	1979	1980	1981	1982	1983	1984
Bordeaux (red)	VG	G	F	VG	G	F	G	VG	VG	F
Bordeaux (white)	VG	G	F	G	G	G	G	G	VG	F
Champagne	VG	VG	P	F	G	G	VG	VG	VG	F
Burgundy (red)	F	G	F	VG	G	F	G	G	VG	F
Burgundy (white)	G	G	F	VG	G	F	VG	G	VG	G
Rhône	P	VG	F	VG	G	G	F	G	VG	G
Italy (red)	G	F	P	VG	VG	G	F	VG	G	G
Alsace	G	VG	P	G	VG	G	VG	VG	VG	F
Spain (reds)	G	G	P	G	F	G	VG	VG	G	F
Germany	—	VG	F	F	G	F	G	G	G	F
California	G	G	G	G	F	G	F	G	F	VG
Port	G	—	VG	—	—	G	—	G	VG	—

(Note: only certain vintages are good enough to be 'declared' in the port region)

W

WACHENHEIM German wine town in the Rheinpfalz, known for its 'soft' white wines.

WASHINGTON STATE American wine region which is improving in quality each year. Once native vines were the rule but now European varieties are more common. The Yakima Valley is the major wine area and **St. Michelle** a major winery.

WEHLEN German wine town in the Mosel. Best-known wine is **Wehlener Sonnenuhr** (Sun Dial).

WEIN Means 'wine' in German.

WEINKELLEREI German for 'wine cellar', can be translated as wine company.

WILTINGEN German wine village in the Mosel region where the **Scharzhofberg** vineyard, maker of exceptional white wines, is located.

WINKEL Notable wine village in the Rheingau, Germany. **Schloss Vollrads** is located here.

WINZERGENOSSENSCHAFT German for 'co-operative' (of wine growers).

WÜRTTEMBERG German region paired with Baden – in the south. Makes red and rosé wine as well as white – the rosé is called **Schillerwein**.

WÜRZBURG Centre of the wine-growing region of Franken, Germany. Known for its **Steinwein** in the flask-shaped bottles.

Y

YAKIMA VALLEY Major wine-growing area in Washington State in the United States.

YQUEM, CHÂTEAU D' Famous sweet white **Sauternes** wine from France. The best and most expensive of this area.

YUGOSLAVIA Best known abroad for its well-made and inexpensive **Riesling,** this country also makes many fine red wines, such as **Dingac** and dessert wines. Major wine areas are Slovenia (for Riesling) and Dalmatia in the south.

Z

ZELL German wine town in the Mosel. It is know for its distinctive wine label the **Zeller Schwarze Katz** (Black Cat).

ZELTINGEN German wine town in the Mosel area. Its best known wine is **Zeltinger Himmelreich** (Heavenly Kingdom).

ZINFANDEL California red grape variety which originated in Italy. It now makes a range of red wines from everyday drinking blends to fine dry wines and even sweet late-harvest 'essence'. **Ridge** is perhaps the finest winery in California for this grape type.

WINE
WITH FOOD

FOOD AND WINE COMBINATIONS

There is no doubt that fine wine will complement and enhance the enjoyment of good food. However, there are many popular misconceptions about what wine is appropriate to what dish, particularly the old adage about reds only going with red meat and whites with white meat. In some wine-producing and indeed great gastronomic regions such as the Rheingau of Germany and Alsace

in France it would, for example, be considered not only normal but correct to drink white wine throughout a meal irrespective of the 'colour' of the meat. There is frankly no hard and fast rule. What is important is what the individual feels suits his or her palate. The suggestions that follow are merely a guide.

Most wine is meant to go with food. Unless the wine in question is very sweet or perhaps fortified, there is a dish somewhere which it is meant to partner. Of course, some wines go well with almost any meal – they are innocuous wines with little character. Most so-called 'generic' wines are this type, as are the wines sold in boxes, cans or bricks.

But what about the finer wines of the world? Here are few ideas for wine 'marriages'.

CONCISE GUIDE

APERITIF WINES: Serve these with canapés or perhaps a simple starter like smoked salmon or paté and toast. Examples are dry **sherry** such as *fino*, dry **Madeira**, **Alsace** wines, light German wines such as those of *Kabinett,* quality, **Champagne** or sparkling wine.

FIRST COURSE: Sherry goes well with soup, espcially consommé. With paté, serve red wine such as **Valpolicella** or **Beaujolais**. With oysters or seafood, **Chablis** is the classic, but **Muscadet, Pouilly-Fumé** or **California Fumé Blanc** also do very well. With richer fish dishes such as soups, serve a fuller white wine like **Gewürztraminer**.

FISH DISHES: All light white wines are suitable, but if there is a cream sauce, then choose something with body like a white **Rioja**, an Italian white wine, or a **Mâcon Blanc**. With a spicy fish dish like Cioppino do not be afraid to offer cool red wine such as **Valpolicella**. Do not serve red wine with oily fish such as mackerel or herring.

POULTRY AND WHITE MEAT: Lovely with **white Burgundy** and **California rosé** or **Cabernet**. With rich fried dishes like escalope, serve a full white wine like **Orvieto**, or a spicy **Riesling** or **Gewürztraminer**.

DUCK OR WILD GAME BIRDS: Serve with **Beaujolais** or a **claret** – a **Rioja** is an interesting alternative, or a good **Chianti**.

LAMB: Can be a little rich, so serve a very 'clean' wine from **Bordeaux**, or a light **Zinfandel**.

HAM: Goes well with white wine such as **Semillon** or **Chardonnay**.

VENISON: All pungent game dishes need a really full red wine like **Rhône red** or perhaps an Australian **Shiraz** or a **California Cabernet Sauvignon.**

BEEF: With roast beef, try a velvety **Burgundy** or a **Pinot Noir** from California. With steak, a spicy **Rhône wine** or **Petite Sirah**, or a claret from **St. Emilion.** Barbecued beef is good with **Zinfandel.**

SALADS: No wine unless you use no dressing – the vinegar or lemon juice will spoil the taste of wine.

PIZZA AND ITALIAN DISHES: **Zinfandel, Chianti** or **Rioja.**

CHINESE DISHES: No wine or perhaps a very little white wine such as **Soave** or **Verdicchio.**

INDIAN DISHES: No wine or a spicy white wine like **Gewürztraminer.**

MILD CHEESE: Serve with a full red wine like **Chardonnay** or **Semillon**, or a light red such as a **Loire Chinon.**

STRONG CHEESE: Blue cheese goes well with **port** or **claret.** Strong French cheese like Camembert blends with **Burgundy** or **Rioja.** Good English-style cheeses such as Cheddar are ideal with aged **claret**, with **Dão** from Portugal, or a full Italian wine like **Barolo.**

PICNIC FOOD: A **rosé** is ideal here. Serve cool, or choose a fruity red such as **Beaujolais** or a fruity white like any **Riesling.**

FRUIT: Apricots with **Muscat de Beaumes de Venise**, raspberries with **Sauternes**, melon with **Colombard** or **Chenin Blanc**, no wine with apples as a rule.

DESSERTS: Wine does not blend with chocolate, but you may want to experiment with sweet **Coteaux du Layon**, or a **Malvasia** from Italy or California with other sugary puddings; no wine with lemon desserts.

AFTER THE MEAL: As an alternative to spirits, offer a **tawny port** or a sweet **Madeira. Cream sherry** is also popular. The French often serve **champagne** with cake after a meal.

WINE AT PARTIES
Use wine at a party with confidence. Tastes are moving towards wine and away from stronger alternatives. For those on diet, mix a fruity wine with soda or a sparkling mineral water to make a spritzer, or mix inexpensive sparkling wine with orange juice to make **Bucks Fizz** (called **Mimosa** in the US). Five measures of mixer to one of wine is about right.

   Spanish **Sangria** is good punch for summer parties. Simply pour a bottle of good red wine, such as **Rioja**, into a bowl or jug and top with double the amount of lemon and orange juice – preferably freshly-squeezed. Add sliced citrus fruit and ice.

WINES FOR SPECIAL MEALS

Matching food with wine is one of the trickiest aspects of wine choice, tied up with wanting to please your guests and at the same time select the 'right' wine for an occasion.
In the following examples of home entertaining, specific wines are matched with typical menus to help guide your choice in a practical way.

E L E G A N T   D I N N E R

With this type of entertaining, the menu is usually fairly rich and impressive. Our example is suitable for 'business' guests or to celebrate in grand style with friends.

Dish	Recommended wine(s)
SOUPE DE POISSON (Fish Soup)	Chablis, Muscadet, Sancerre, Soave.
GIGOT RÔTI (Roast Lamb)	A light red Burgundy such as Volnay or Mercurey; Chianti; Rioja; California Pinot Noir.
SALADE (Green Salad)	If dressed with vinaigrette, serve mineral water – if you use lemon juice only, then a little more of the red or white wines.
FROMAGES (e.g. Brie, Cheddar and Stilton)	Red Bordeaux; Côtes du Rhône; Corbières or Minervois; Bulgarian Cabernet Sauvignon; California Zinfandel.
TARTE NORMANDE (Apple Tart)	Monbazillac; Coteaux du Layon; Italian Moscato; Australian Muscat.

QUANTITIES (for six): 1 bottle of the dry white wine selected; 2 bottles of red wine to accompany main course and the cheese; one bottle of sweet white wine. It is worth having extra stock of all but the sweet wine as some guests may not like red wine at all, or prefer one particular wine throughout the meal. Always offer water during this type of rich meal and especially between wines, and after the salad course.

(for eight people)

INFORMAL LUNCH
PARTY

This might be a gathering on a Saturday or during the week without too much ceremony. The wine reflects this style.

Dish	Recommended wine(s)
COLD MEATS AND PATÉS	Beaujolais; Valpolicella; rosé wines. Or choose a light German wine for anyone who prefers white wine.
RISOTTO (with salads)	
CHEESE & FRESH FRUITS	

QUANTITIES: (for eight) 4 bottles of your selected wine. One at least should be a white wine so you can offer a choice. An additional option is to serve a single glass of sweetish wine such as **Muscat de Beaumes de Venise** with the fruit or after the meal as a 'digestif'.

(for approximately 20 people)

B U F F E T   S U P P E R

This type of event is a useful way of saying 'thank you' to
colleagues, neighbours or acquaintances without endless dinner
parties. As this is a cross between a cocktail party and a dinner party
the wine should be plentiful and therefore not too expensive.

Dish	Recommended wine(s)
GRILLED CHICKEN LEGS	This is a perfect time to try both
COLD ROAST BEEF WITH SAUCES	red and white *Vins de Pays* from France e.g. white **Bergerac** and a red **Côtes du Roussillon**; or a
MARINATED MUSHROOMS	large bottle or two from Italy e.g.
CUCUMBERS IN SOUR CREAM	**Valpolicella** (light red) or
BREADS	**Frascati** (dry white); a medium-dry Riesling such as **Lutomer**
CHEESE BOARD	from Yugoslavia would be a
STRAWBERRY BAVAROIS (cream)	good alternative for any guest who does not enjoy a very dry wine.

QUANTITIES: For about 20 people buy one case (12 bottles) of
wine (or its equivalent in larger bottles). This could be made up of 6
each of red and white French *Vin de Pays*; 4 Frascati and 2
Valpolicella in 1.5 litre bottles; or 4 Lutomer, 4 dry white and 4 red,
according to your guests' preferences. Offer mineral water,
preferably sparkling, and include some fresh fruit juices in your
shopping.

BARBECUE PARTY

During the summer when the weather is fine, a barbecue is the ideal way to entertain. All formality may be dispensed with and even paper plates and plastic (clear) tumblers can be used. This is a particularly suitable time to try all those 'convenience' wines offered in supermarkets and wine shops.

Dish	Recommended wine(s)
GRILLED SPICY SAUSAGES GRILLED STEAK GRILLED MARINADED CHICKEN RICE SALAD TOMATO SALAD FRESH FRUIT CHOCOLATE CAKE	This is a good time to offer a slightly sparkling rosé such as **Mateus Rosé** – it tastes best outdoors. Or offer a light low alcohol wine such as **Vinho Verde** from Portugal, with perhaps some **Dão** red wine from that country for those who like red wine with their steak. If using a wine 'box' ensure you keep the white wine well chilled or it may taste 'oily' and not as pleasant as it should. **Note:** no wine with chocolate cake!

QUANTITIES: For eight people allow a half-bottle of wine per person, or even a little more if you are offering wine in a 'box' or a low alcohol wine such as Vinho Verde. Beware of offering too much heavy red wine outdoors on a sunny day. One or two alternative bottles of Dão and a greater amount of a light red (such as **Beaujolais** in a box), plus plenty of white wine and mineral water should suffice.

(for six people)

E N G L I S H   P I C N I C

This is the type of fantasy picnic from days gone by, still recreated in Britain and in other parts of the world on special social occasions. Extravagance is the keynote – if you can't afford an expensive hamper, extend yourself with the wine and choose some real champagne (at least to begin with).

Dish	Recommended wine(s)
SMOKED SALMON	Good dry **champagne** or sparkling wine or real white Burgundy, such as **Meursault**.
COLD ROAST PARTRIDGE OR QUAIL	Good claret such as a classed wine from the Médoc (e.g. **Château Lynch-Bages** or **Château Talbot**); or a **Rioja Reserva**.
SALADS/CHEESE including Stilton	Continue with the red wine.
CHAMPAGNE SORBET	A medium-dry **champagne** (demi-sec) or **Asti Spumante**.

QUANTITIES: For six, allow one bottle dry wine/champagne, two bottles red, one bottle medium-dry champagne/sparkling wine.

CASUAL GREEK MEAL

This is a very casual and relaxed meal with good friends who like hearty fare and simple country wines. It has a Greek influence and might bright back holiday memories.

Dish	Recommended wine(s)
LEMON SOUP	Serve **Retsina** if available and if you think your friends have tried it before — it has an unusual taste which does complement food cooked in olive oil. With the Moussaka offer either a red Greek or Cyprus wine such as **Othello** or **Demestica**; or a full red from the Rhône Valley such as **Châteauneuf-du-Pape**; or a **Barbera** from Italy or California. The ideal wine with melon is **Colombard** from California, South Africa or Australia.
MOUSSAKA	
GARLIC BREAD	
TOMATO SALAD with feta cheese	
MELON	

QUANTITIES: For six allow a half bottle per person (1 of Retsina, 2 red). If you plan to serve a wine with the melon (not essential) then this one bottle is extra. Finish with a glass of **Metaxa** (Greek brandy) for an authentic touch with coffee.

(for ten people)

F E S T I V E   D I N N E R

This is the typical Christmas meal, or perhaps a Thanksgiving dinner in the US. The food is rich and needs light wine to counterbalance it.

Dish	Recommended wine(s)
VICHYSOISSE (Chilled leek/ potato soup)	*Fino* **sherry** or light **Madeira** (chilled).
ROAST TURKEY, stuffing, sausages BREAD SAUCE VEGETABLES/SALAD	**Riesling** from Germany or Yugoslavia; **Gewürztraminer** or **Riesling** from Alsace if a drier wine is preferred; **Beaujolais** for red wine lovers.
CHRISTMAS PUDDING or Pumpkin Pie	**Asti Spumanti** or sweet **champagne**.

QUANTITIES: For a family of ten allow a bottle per person for this long protracted meal; 2 bottles of sherry or Madeira (more if offering as an aperitif beforehand); 6 bottles of the main wine selection, including 1 or 2 of Beaujolais if you know you have some red wine lovers; 2 bottles of sweet wine. And plan to rest afterwards!

WINE AND CHEESE PARTY

This traditional and inexpensive type of gathering is a good way to try unusual wines. Alternatively, why not propose everyone brings a bottle, perhaps from a particular country or region?

Dish	Recommended wine(s)
CHEESES should include GOAT CHEESE (Chèvre)	Full white wine such as **white Mâcon** or **Burgundy**, or **California Chardonnay**.
BLUE CHEESE (e.g. Stilton, Dolcelatte, Roquefort)	Good with white as above or with sweet **Sauternes** or **Barsac**.
SOFT CHEESE (e.g. Brie, Bel Paese, Boursin)	A light red wine such as **claret** or **Chianti**.
HARD CHEESE (e.g. Cheddar, Cantal, Parmesan)	Full red wine such as red **Burgundy** or a **Rioja**.

QUANTITIES: Allow a half bottle per person, with some in reserve. As a rule most people prefer red wine with cheese, although the pleasures of goat cheese, for instance, with a white wine might be a new experience.

(for 2 persons)

CELEBRATION DINNER

This might be the type of seductive meal for two planned for an anniversary or perhaps Valentine's Day. It owes its style to *nouvelle cuisine* and wines should be very subtle to match the food.

Dish	Recommended wine(s)
INDIVIDUAL FRESH TOMATO SOUFFLES	French white Burgundy such as **Montrachet** or a **Mâcon Villages**; California Chardonnay.
STUFFED CHICKEN BREASTS WITH VARIOUS VEGETABLE PURÉES	Red wine from the Loire, such as **Chinon**; good **Beaujolais**; Bardolino.
HOME-MADE WALNUT ICE CREAM	**Champagne** or sparkling wine, or a glass of good **tawny port**, served chilled.

QUANTITIES: For a modest celebration, allow ½ bottle white wine, 1 bottle red and ½ bottle champagne. More lavishly, drink a full bottle of champagne; or alternatively have ½ bottle champagne as an aperitif and a glass of tawny port as a digestif.

GLASSWARE

As a general rule, a wine glass should be transparent and have a stem. Its shape may owe something to tradition but your choice will often depend on the use you intend for it. A tasting glass, for example, has a 'tulip' shape so that the full aroma of the wine may be appreciated. On the other hand, for a dinner party you may prefer some elegant cut-glass to match your table setting.

STYLES OF GLASSES

Tasting glass (1) is mid-sized and the bowl curves in slightly. It has a stem and the taster avoids touching the bowl – swirl your sample holding the base or stem. Do not overfill, as a mere half-inch (3.5cl) of wine is a typical sample; **White wine glasses** (2) usually resemble the tasting glass but may have regional variations such as a

round bowl and coloured stem for Alsace and German wine. Rhine wines, for example, are often served in brown-stemmed glasses while Mosel and Alsace are offered in glasses with green stems (3); **Red wine glasses** (4) may be in a larger tulip shape or goblets (traditional to Burgundy). Be careful not to overfill a large goblet – some contain half a bottle when full. The so-called 'Paris goblet' (5) is used in bars and restaurants and makes a useful everyday glass at home; Rosé wines (6) are served in any style you prefer to show their attractive colour. The **flûte glass** (7) is the classic style for champagne. The tall, slim shape displays the bubbles to advantage and means they last longer than in the old-fashioned 'coupe' glass. Fortified wines (8) are obviously served in smaller measures. Sherry is served in a traditional **copita** (9) which has an exaggerated tulip shape. This may also be used for port. Avoid tiny liqueur-type glasses as the aroma will be lost.

ACCESSORIES

Corkscrews When choosing a corkscrew, make sure the screw part is firmly attached. One of the easiest types to use, especially if you are confronted with a very ancient cork, is the Screwpull, an American invention; or try the two-pronged style made in Germany.

Ice bucket Serving wine at the correct temperature is important. To maintain white wine and sparkling wines at the correct level, use an ice bucket filled with a mixture of ice and water.

Decanters Wine in large bottles or boxes may be served more readily in an attractive glass carafe or stoneware pitcher (called a *pichet* in France). For more elegant vintages (of red wine and port) try to use a clear glass decanter, rather than one of cut or coloured glass, so that you can show off the subtle shade of the wine. These wines should be steadily decanted in a good light until you see the sediment. Filter the remainder through coffee papers if the wine is really special.

Wine racks For storage, ensure your chosen rack is really solidly made so that the bottles vibrate as little as possible. All wines with corks must be kept lying on one side and undisturbed before drinking. The racks made with metal and wood are very practical. For large quantities, store wines in 'open bins' with each clearly marked. Make sure you keep a record of the wines in your 'cellar'. Use a notebook or buy a special cellar book if you wish. This can be not only a practical aid to what you have bought and drunk, but also an interesting record of when, and with what, you served certain wines.

WINE CLASSIFICATIONS

CLASSIFICATION OF BORDEAUX WINES

1855 OFFICIAL CLASSIFICATION OF THE WINES OF THE MÉDOC

RED WINES

1er cru classé (2nd growth)

Château	Commune
Ch. Lafite	*Pauillac*
Ch. Latour	*Pauillac*
Ch. Margaux	*Margaux*
Ch. Haut-Brion	*Graves*
Ch. Mouton-Rothschild	*Pauillac*
(elevated to Premier Cru	
by Presidential decree 1973)	

2e cru classé (2nd growth)

Ch. Rausan-Ségla	*Margaux*
Ch. Rauzan-Gassies	*Margaux*
Ch. Léoville-Las-Cases	*St Julien*
Ch. Léoville-Poyferré	*St Julien*
Ch. Léoville-Barton	*St Julien*
Ch. Durfort-Vivens	*Margaux*
Ch. Lascombes	*Margaux*
Ch. Gruaud-Larose	*St Julien*
Ch. Brane-Cantenac	*Margaux*
Ch. Pichon-Longueville	*Pauillac*
Ch. Pichon-Longueville-Lalande	*Pauillac*
Ch. Ducru-Beaucaillou	*St Julien*
Ch. Cos d'Estournel	*St Estèphe*
Ch. Montrose	*St Estèphe*

3e cru classé (3rd growth)

Ch. Kirwan	*Margaux*
Ch. d'Issan	*Margaux*
Ch. Lagrange	*St Julien*
Ch. Langoa	*St Julien*
Ch. Giscours	*Margaux*
Ch. Malescot-St-Exupéry	*Margaux*
Ch. Cantenac-Brown	*Margaux*
Ch. Palmer	*Margaux*
Ch. Lagune	*Haut Médoc*
Ch. Desmirail	*Margaux*
Ch. Calon-Ségur	*St Estèphe*
Ch. Ferrière	*Margaux*
Ch. Marquis d'Alesme-Becker	*Margaux*
Ch. Boyd-Cantenac	*Margaux*

	Château	Commune
4ᵉ cru classé (4th growth)		

Château	Commune
Ch. St-Pierre-Seviastre	*St Julien*
Ch. St-Pierre-Bontemps	*St Julien*
Ch. Branaire-Ducru	*St Julien*
Ch. Talbot	*St Julien*
Ch. Duhart-Milon	*Pauillac*
Ch. Pouget	*Margaux*
Ch. La Tour-Carnet	*Haut Médoc*
Ch. Lafon-Rochet	*St Estèphe*
Ch. Beychevelle	*St Julien*
Ch. Prieuré-Lichine	*Margaux*
Ch. Marquis-de-Terme	*Margaux*

5ᵉ cru classé (5th growth)

Château	Commune
Ch. Pontet-Canet	*Pauillac*
Ch. Batailley	*Pauillac*
Ch. Haut-Batailley	*Pauillac*
Ch. Grande-Puy-Lacoste	*Pauillac*
Ch. Grande-Puy-Ducasse	*Pauillac*
Ch. Lynch-Bages	*Pauillac*
Ch. Lynch-Moussas	*Pauillac*
Ch. Dauzac	*Margaux*
Ch. Mouton-Baronne-Philippe	*Pauillac*
Ch. du Tertre	*Margaux*
Ch. Haut-Bages-Libéral	*Pauillac*
Ch. Pédesclaux	*Pauillac*
Ch. Belgrave	*Haut Médoc*
Ch. Camensac	*Haut Médoc*
Ch. Cos Labory	*St Estèphe*
Ch. Clerc-Milon	*Pauillac*
Ch. Croizet-Bages	*Pauillac*
Ch. Cantemerle	*Haut Médoc*

ST ÉMILION 1954 OFFICIAL CLASSIFICATION

PREMIERS GRANDS CRUS CLASSÉS

A

Châteaux
Ausone
Cheval-Blanc

B

Beauséjour
Bélair
Canon
Clos Fourtet
Figeac
La Gaffelière
Magdelaine
Pavie
Trottevieille

1855 CLASSIFICATION OF SAUTERNES AND BARSAC

Châteaux	Communes
GRAND PREMIER CRU	
d'Yquem	Sauternes
PREMIERS CRUS	
La Tour-Blanche	Bommes
Lafaurie-Peyraguey	Bommes
Clos Haut-Peyraguey	Bommes
Rayne-Vigneau	Bommes
Suduiraut	Preignac
Coutet	Barsac
Climens	Barsac
Guiraud	Sauternes
Rieussec	Fargues
Sigalas-Rabaud	Bommes
Rabaud-Promis	Bommes
DEUXIÉMES CRUS	
Myrat	Barsac
Doisy-Dubroca	Barsac
Doisy-Daëne	Barsac
Doisy-Védrines	Barsac
d'Arche	Sauternes
Pexoto	Sauternes
Filhot	Bommes
Broustet	Barsac
Nairac	Barsac
Caillou	Barsac
Suau	Barsac
de-Malle	Preignac
Romer	Fargues
Romer-Du-Hayot	Fargues
Lamothe	Sauternes

Information provided by Food and Wine from France, 41-46 Piccadilly, London W1.

BURGUNDY GRANDS CRUS

CHABLIS GRANDS CRUS

Vaudésir
Les Clos
Grenouilles
Valmur
Blanchots
Preuses
Bougros

BURGUNDY GRANDS CRUS (Red wines unless otherwise stated)

Côte de Nuits   *indicates superior *grands crus*

Commune

Gevrey-Chambertin *Chambertin
     *Chambertin-Clos-de-Bèze
     Chapelle-Chambertin
     Charmes-Chambertin
     Griottes-Chambertin
     Latricières-Chambertin
     Mazis-Chambertin
     Mazoyères-Chambertin
     Ruchottes-Chambertin

Morey-St-Denis *Bonnes-Mares (also in Chambolle-Musigny)
     *Clos-de-la-Roche
     *Clos-de-Tart (also in Chambolle-Musigny)
     *Clos-des-Lambrays

Chambolle-Musigny *Musigny (including some white wine)

Vougeot *Clos-de-Vougeot

Vosne-Romanée *Echézeaux
     *Grands-Echézeaux
     *La Tâche
     *Richebourg
     *Romanée-Conti
     *Romanée-St-Vivant

Côte de Beaune

Commune

Aloxe-Corton *Corton
     *Corton-Charlemagne (white wine only)

Puligny-Montrachet
Montrachet
(white wines only) *Montrachet (white wines only)
     *Chevalier-Montrachet
     Bâtard-Montrachet
     Bienvenues-Bâtard-Montrachet
     Criots-Bâtard-Montrachet

Information from: Fédération des interprofessions viticoles de Grande
Bourgogne et Direction générale des impôts.

INDEX

See also WINES AND VINES Dictionary
pages 70-133

Editor: Jennifer Mulherin
Designer and Art Director: Tom Deas

Acknowledgements
The publishers would like to thank the
following individuals and organizations for
their help in producing this book:
Australian Trade Commission, London;
Anthony Barne, The Cocktail
Shop, 30 Neal St, Covent Garden,
London WC2; Con Creek Winery, Napa
County, California; Covent Garden Kitchen
Supplies, London; David Mellor Design
Ltd, James St, London WC2; Del Monico,
64 Old Compton St, London W1;
Dolamore Ltd, 15 Craven Road,
London W2; Food and Wine from France,
London; German Wine Information
Centre, London; Italian Trade Centre,
London; Peter Morrell, Morrell and Co,
New York City; Joseph Phelps Vineyards,
Napa County, California; Sebastini
Vineyards, Sonoma County, California;
Spanish Wine Information Centre,
London; Trefethen Vineyards, Napa
County, California; Wine Cart, New York
City; Wine Institute of California,
San Francisco.

Picture credits
Special photography: Graham Young
Stylist: Lyn Rutherford
Maps: James Macdonald

Australian Trade Commission, 73; Simon
Butcher 22, 50/1, 59; French Food Wine
11, 15, 17, 21, 71, 77, 80, 82, 83, 86, 88/9, 90,
97, 105, 106, 109, 120, 123, 124, 125, 128,
131, 138; German Wine Information 93,
101, 118; Italian Trade Centre 31, 52, 62,
64/5, 84, 99, 114, 115, 130, 136; Charles
Nicholas 2/3, 8/9, 111; Spanish Wine
Information Centre 25, 28, 63, 100, 116,
121, 126, 127, 134/5.